Conquer Your Purpose

First Printed in Great Britain by
Obex Publishing Ltd in 2020

2 4 6 8 10 9 7 5 3 1

Copyright Jean-Claude Leveque, 2020

Jean-Claude Leveque has asserted his right under the Copyright, Designs and Patents Act 1988 to be identified as the author of this work.

All rights reserved. No parts of this publication may be reproduced, stored in a retrieval system, or transmitted in any form or by any means, electronic, mechanical, photocopying, recording or otherwise, without the prior permission of the copyright owner.

Paperback ISBN   978-1-913454-13-5
eBook ISBN   978-1-913454-14-2

A CIP catalogue record for this book is available from the British Library.

Obex Publishing Ltd.
Reg. No. 12169917

CONTENTS

INTRODUCTION 5

CHAPTER 1: WHAT IS YOUR PURPOSE RIGHT NOW? 8

CHAPTER 2: PUT DOWN THE GPS AND START REWRITING YOUR OWN JOURNEY 19

CHAPTER 3: THE IMPORTANCE OF PLANNING 32

CHAPTER 4: IF AT FIRST YOU DON'T SUCCEED 46

CHAPTER 5: THE POWER OF YOUR OWN MIND 65

CHAPTER 6: WHAT COMES NEXT? 94

CHAPTER 7: WILL YOUR PURPOSE FULFIL YOU COMPLETELY? 107

BONUS CHAPTER: MOTIVATION SUMMARY 101 119

CONCLUSION 136

Introduction

Life is for living; that's a truth.

Life is also extremely short, another truth.

So, do you actually like where you are right now? Is your current destination a pitstop on your way to greatness, or do you feel like you're completely lost somewhere without a compass to guide you?

From time to time in life, it is completely normal to feel a little lost, but the key is to make sure you know this and make changes before you go from a little lost to completely wandering around in the dark with no clue what your own name is.

Life throws us curveballs and it's very easy to simply settle with what we have, assuming that we're happy, but it's only when you look back, probably when you're old and grey, that you realise you missed the mark by miles.

As a result, you're left with regret and aims you wish you'd tried a little harder to reach.

That's a common story, but it's not one that has to be yours.

Whether you're 21, 81, or anything in-between (or maybe older), it's never too late to change your direction and move towards something that you really covet in life. Whether that's changing your career and retraining completely from scratch, or looking to buy a house overseas and saving up for a deposit first, the subject matter doesn't necessarily matter, but the fact that you're making steps towards achieving it does.

This book is going to challenge your current situation in life. It's going to help you look back and decide whether you're comfortable with your current destination or whether you wish it was somewhere else entirely.

At first, it might feel uncomfortable, because you might be faced with the reality that you wish you'd taken a completely different path in life. That's okay, but it's important you allow yourself to feel that realisation in order to ensure that you don't become complacent and remain in your comfort zone.

It was Neale Donald Walsch who said that "life begins at the end of your comfort zone" and there has never been a truer word said. Life isn't designed to be easy or super-comfortable, it's supposed to challenge you, and it's supposed to make you strive for more. You can't be expected to make powerful changes in life without feeling a little of the fear and doing it anyway. Another rather wonderful quote right there!

So, this book is going to push you and make you think. Once you've thought about it, we're going to help you develop a new journey, one which will take you where you want to go, and one which will allow you to reach the aims and dreams you have in life, without having to sit back and wish you'd tried a little bit harder, somewhere down the line.

We're going to identify your purpose, then we're going to follow a series of analogies that take your purpose and turn it into a road-trip journey. There will be scenic routes and there will be boring motorway sections, there might be bumps in the road and occasionally you might end up with a flat tyre, but with a little perseverance, a little road-side assistance occasionally and a good quality map, i.e. your own desire, you'll get to where you want to be in the end. You might run out of gas occasionally, but remember, there is always a station not too far away.

So, grab your flask and a blanket, we're about to get into the car and fasten our seatbelts. We guarantee this is going to be the ride of your life!

Chapter 1:
What is Your Purpose Right Now?

Depending upon which source you try, there are a couple of different definitions for the word "purpose". They are:

"The reason for which something is done or created or for which something exists."
"A person's sense of resolve or determination."

So, using those two definitions which link together very well, what is your purpose in life?

The fact you have picked up this book tells us that you might not actually have one at this point. That's fine because that means the book is going to be very useful to you and may just change the path of your life for the better.

For the, pardon the pun, proposes of this book, a purpose is a reason for doing something. So, that means you need an aim and a purpose in order to make the whole thing work. Which comes first? It's almost a chicken and the egg kind of situation, but first, you need the aim in many ways, because that then informs you of why you're doing it. Or, perhaps you know why you want something, you're just not sure what is going to get you there. In that case, you have the purpose before the aim.

If you have a clue what your purpose or your aim is at this moment, you need to sit down and do a spot of careful thinking. The good news is that you have plenty of time and you only need a slight inkling to get started. The rest of the book will guide you through the process of turning a small idea into something great.

If you do have a purpose right now, it's a good idea to jot it down somewhere. If you have an idea, jot that down. At this point, basically do a quick brainstorming session of anything that pops into your mind, which may inform your purpose or your aim. That is your key starting point.

Creating Your Life's Journey

There are not many people who know what they want in life from a young age. There is certainly social pressure to know, but if you surveyed a large group of people, a very considerable selection would tell you that they have no idea what they want to do and didn't have a clue at a young age either. We're basically drifting through life with no clear aim and therefore no purpose. We are on a journey to literally nowhere. We're lost, bumping from place to place and about to run out of petrol.

That's never a good thing!

Your journey begins the day you are born, but you cannot make headway into your real midsection until you're old enough to know what you want to do. That point can come when you're 14; it can come when you're 50, it might not come until you're almost 70. Many of us also have several different ideas which we assume to be our focal point, but as we start on the way towards reaching them, we decide that we didn't give it enough thought in the end and we change direction once more.

It might also be that you had an idea and it was a good one, but you hit a roadblock, and rather than trying to traverse your way around it or calling for help, you gave up and decided to walk in another direction.

The point here is that your life's journey is full of twists and turns, but if you want something badly enough, you have to be prepared to do the planning and do the hard work.

Before we get into the hard work of trying to figure out your exact purpose, although we've already urged you to write down a few ideas if you have any, you need to first acknowledge where you are right now. Again, write it down in the most simplistic way you can think of, as we're going to unpick this as we move through the first few chapters.

So, if you're currently working as a nurse and you have dreams to travel one day, write it down. If you're a footballer, write it down. At this point you don't have to add your dreams to it, but if any crop up, scribble them down.

You Believe What You See

If most of us don't have a clue what we want in life until we're a lot older than we're "supposed" to know, what does that really mean? Does it mean that we believe the things we see when we're younger and we grow and assume that happiness is simply 'being'?

For some people, that is the meaning of true happiness, and if that's you right now, well done. In that case, you might not need this book at all! However, the chances are that there are at least elements of your life you're not so happy with.

We believe the things that are in front of us and we're not told to challenge or attempt to change them. Why? Because they're there in front of our eyes, so they must be true! The thing is, somethings are nothing more than an illusion, and because you can see them in physical form, you might completely misinterpret their meaning.

Life is a little deeper than the things you simply have in front of you, and by taking things at face value, you're missing out on some very empowering and enlightening details.

For instance, you might see a junior doctor working in a hospital and assume that he is living his best life. He has a high flying job and he gets to help people every day. That is your assumption and it turns into fact in your mind. However, when you scratch the surface, you find out that he actually never wanted to become a doctor and he was pushed into it by his parents. He's been working 50 hour weeks for the past month and he's absolutely exhausted, wishing he had gone for his initial dream of being a pro surfer all those years ago.

Things are rarely as cut and dried as we assume, and that goes for the things you want in life too.

You might look at a dream career you have had your eye on for a long time and assume that it's going to be everything you've ever wanted, but have you done your research? Have you actually sat down and Googled the life out of it, unpicking the small details and trying to work out whether or not it will be what you want?

Whilst you're trying to work out what your purpose is, be sure to do some research and keep an open mind. Things are not always as they seem and although we do believe what we see, it's important to be open-minded too.

Where Did Your Current Journey Come From?

How did you end up on the journey you're on? Whether you like where you are or not, you're on a journey of some kind. So, how did you get there? Did you take a wrong turning? Were you placed on the journey due to social or parental pressure? Did you simply start off on one route and somehow got lost, taking another turning that took you down a completely random road?

Social and familiar pressures are quite common and these date back for centuries. For instance, there have been jobs that have traditionally be done by men and women, yet these days any gender can do them. Certain cultures try and encourage their children to go into a certain career, such as the medical field or teaching, and that child might not want to, yet feels pressured to do so.

The same goes for the traditional idea of women getting married and having children at a certain age.

Perhaps you found yourself pregnant at an early age and as such, your journey took a slight detour. What you need to understand that is pressures from outside influences can derail your life and the purpose that you have, but it's never too late to get it back on track. If you did end up having a family far younger than you ever planned, you have a second chance to re-start your purpose right now.

Identifying where your current journey came from might seem a little odd, but it is designed to help you understand whether or not it was forced upon you by an invisible pressure, or whether you chose it and simply didn't put enough effort and planning into the decision.

By this point, you should know what your journey is, i.e. where you are now, where that journey originated from, and you might also have a slight idea about your purpose, although equally, you might not have got that far. The first two are enough for now!

Do You Like Your Journey's Current Location?

Okay, next point. Taking your current journey into account, do you like where it is going? Or, possibly more likely, do you have likes and dislikes about the entire thing?

It's not that you don't dislike your current journey completely, but it's also possible that there are certain points you would like to change. Your next task is to work out the parts of your journey that you like currently and those you would like to change. By doing that, you can incorporate the good parts into your new journey, and you can work to cut out the parts that you're not a fan of when you redesign your new route.

However, the fact that you're reading a book about finding your purpose and rewriting your life's story tells us that there enough parts of your journey which you want to change, otherwise you probably wouldn't have even entertained changing anything about where you are right now.

Why Are You Attached to Where You Are Now?

The final point we need to talk about before it's time to get practical and start thinking about the future is the very reason why you have stayed on the journey you're on.

You're comfortable.

Now, comfortable is, well, comfortable, but does that mean it's going to give you what you want in the end? Probably not.

You're not going to achieve anything wonderful whilst you're stuck in your comfort zone. The reason is that whilst your comfort zone is exactly that, comfortable; it's a zone for a reason; you need to get out of certain zones in order to impress. When you stay somewhere, or in something, because it's comfortable, you're never stretching yourself and never giving yourself the opportunity to work out what you're truly capable of doing. That means your potential remains untapped and your life simply ticks along at the same pace, never really picking up speed, or working through the regular peaks and troughs that normal life does.

Again, the fact you've picked up this book tells us that you're not completely attached to where you are; otherwise, the entire process of reading a book would be a complete waste of time. However, if you're stuck where you are because you're scared of reaching outside of your comfort zone and you're worried about what might happen when you try something you've never attempted before, it's time to be brave and take a giant leap into the great unknown.

Points to Take From This Chapter

This chapter has been quite the pep talk, but it's needed to help guide you towards what comes next - a brave step into the unknown.

Do not feel negative or bad about the fact that you have had to come to this point, because nobody is without fault in life. We're all guilty of staying with something out of comfort, and it's only a true problem when you stay there and don't think about moving simply because you're scared.

Your journey to date may not be leading you towards your final destination, as there might be new twists and turns to come.

However, the main points to take from this chapter are:

- Your purpose is the thing which means something to you, something you want to achieve
- Your aim is your destination, although it may not be your final destination
- Your journey can and will change throughout your lifetime
- Most people have no idea what they want to do with their life by the time they're "supposed" to know
- It's not always a good idea to simply believe what you see, as often there is an illusion at hand
- Some people are coerced into a lifestyle because it is what society expects of them, or their family have certain expectations
- It's never too late to make a change.

Chapter 2:
Put Down The GPS And Start Rewriting Your Own Journey

In the last chapter, we talked about what your purpose is and why it's totally fine to not know right at the start what it is. As you brainstorm and think a little, you'll find a route that you like the sound of, and that will set you on your way.

In this chapter, we're going to talk about how to start creating your new journey and the elements that you need to consider as you do so. This chapter is therefore designed to help you come to a conclusion on what your new journey is going to entail. You might not have a solid aim in place, but you will know the direction in which you want to go, and that will allow you to make further headway.

First things first, you have to realise that where you are now is not on your new map, you're about to create a brand new GPS system, compass, map, or whatever method of finding the way you normally use!

Your Current Place is Off The Map

Where you are now is not what you are aiming for. Again, the fact you've picked up this book means you need a change. That means you need a totally new direction and you need to throw your old map in the bin.

The likelihood, however, is that you ever had a map in the first place and that you've simply been coasting from place to place, not really understanding what you're supposed to do, or what you want. That is all about to change, but first, you need to make a commitment to yourself.

If you want to make this change, you need to be truly ready to do it. Sure, you might not know for certain where you're going at this point in time, but you need to focus on the fact you're going somewhere. Promise yourself you're going to go for it, and you're going to continue going until you reach a point where you either want to change direction once more (totally possible) or you've reached where you finally want to go.

Accept that your current position isn't going to feature on your new map. You're leaving behind disappointment, upset, and regrets and you're going to design a brand new journey. That requires commitment and effort, however.

Are you ready to go for it?

What Elements of Your Current Journey do You Want to Keep?

We're not contradicting here, but what parts of your current journey do you want to keep when you design your new one? You don't have to keep a lot, but there are likely to be one or two points of your life that you quite like, or which remind you of something special to you. In that case, it's totally fine if you don't want to deviate completely.

However, make sure that this is kept to a minimum; otherwise you're going to end up simply repeating history and ending upon the same route.

Grab a piece of paper and write down the elements of your life that you really like right now and which you wouldn't like to change. Be careful in what you write down otherwise you could simply end up going down the line of "it's all very comfortable, I think I'll stay here".

If you like your current location and you don't want to move to another town or city, that's fine, you can simply work from where you are. If you like your job, but you want to move locations, that's something you can look to do. You don't have to change every single little thing, but if you're going to embrace your purpose in life, you do need to be prepared to make significant changes that will allow new energy to enter into your space, wherever that may be.

Common Mistakes to Avoid When Designing Your New Route

By now, we're assuming that you've identified your journey's purpose, and you're working on figuring out how to get there.

Great news.

Now, you need to know about a few specific mistakes which are often made when it comes to designing a new journey route. People have walked the same road before you and made the mistakes, so you don't have to. The good news is that you can learn about those mistakes and make sure you don't repeat them whilst designing your new route.

Mistake 1 - Staying Within Your Comfort Zone

We've talked about the comfort zone a little already, and we've mentioned that a certain part of you might want to stay within it because it's soft, squidgy, comfortable, and it helps you sleep at night.

There is no room for soft and squidgy when redesigning your life!

The single biggest mistake you can make when designing your new route, and probably the most common mistake too, is staying within your comfort zone or telling yourself that you're doing something but in reality you're simply staying where you are and tweaking the smallest changes to disguise your fear of doing something different.

Remember, you have already made a promise to yourself that you're going to work hard and go for it - don't back out now!

We do understand, your comfort zone is something you've been used to for so long that it's so familiar. Stepping just one toe outside of its perimeter gives you the shakes; we get it really we do. The problem is, by not stepping a foot outside, you're not allowing yourself the full scope of the experience, and as a result, it's all just going to fail rather drastically, leaving you right back where you started.

Mistake 2 - Not Taking The Time to Really Solidify Your Purpose

Don't even think about taking one step on this journey you're considering without first solidifying and being sure about your journey. This isn't something you should go into half-heartedly, but it's a common mistake to be so excited about changing something that you want to jump straight in and get on with it.

Your excitement and anticipation are admirable, it really is, but your journey isn't going to work unless you're sure of what you want and you've really made a firm decision to go for it.

Developing and following a new journey is something you need to decide upon clearly before you take any action, so despite the excitement of something shiny and new, try and rein in your excitement until you have all the details laid out clearly.

Mistake 3 - Going Along With Someone Else's Idea

When you're not really sure what you want, it's easy to go along with someone else's idea because it seems like a good one. The thing is, that's their journey and it's not yours. You're not going to enjoy or get the most out of a journey that was never designed for you.

Whilst there is nothing wrong with looking at someone else's idea and perhaps wondering whether certain elements of it will work alongside what you're planning, it is totally wrong to basically steal it completely. Maybe "steal" is the wrong word, but going along with something because you're not sure of your own path isn't the right reason to do so. instead, just put some more effort into working out what you want and try and take it slowly if you're not sure.

Mistake 4 - Not Doing Your Research

Another huge mistake is not doing enough research before jumping into your plan with both feet. You need to work out the small details if you want this to work, and that's something we're going to explore in more detail in a later chapter.

Your research forms the basis of your plan and that means you can easily move forward with confidence, knowing that the information you've based your plan on isn't going to fall through and leave you flat on your back on the floor.

Research isn't something you should rush, and you should also make sure that you use reliable sources to obtain it. You can't be sure that where you're getting an entire lot of information from is reliable if you don't check things out and compare. It might also be useful to ask for advice from those close to you who might have knowledge of the area you're trying to move into.

Mistake 5 - Making Assumptions

As part of the research process comes a warning - do not make assumptions! You might think you know how something works, or you know what to do, but you've never walked this path before, so how can you be sure?

You can't!

Making assumptions means that you're guessing basically, you're walking around with your eyes closed, trying to feel the way with your hands. It will end in disaster because this is a journey that requires careful management and the correct information on which to base it all. If you simply assume you know something and just work on that, you're probably going to notice mistakes coming your way.

Mistake 6 - Thinking Too Big

We don't want to rein in your dreams here, because it's important to have a big plan, but thinking too big initially isn't the best idea. Baby steps will get you to where you need to go, and if you get the chance to make a leap forward, it will come when it is ready. Simply launching yourself forwards and thinking you can conquer the world in one sitting is a recipe for disaster and the more trouble you run into, the more you're going to be discouraged from continuing with your plan.

So, have a large plan in mind, but don't go for it all at once. Take small, manageable steps and you'll notice that your progress is far easier and swift than it would otherwise be. Rome certainly wasn't built in a day!

Mistake 7 - Assuming That You Know it All

You might have done your research to a certain degree, in fact, you might have done a lot of it, but you do not know it all and probably never will! Arrogance will get you into trouble when trying to plot a new course in life and if you want to find your purpose and really take it to the next level you need to be sure in your aim, but you also need to be humble enough to accept that you're not going to know everything.

Find a mentor who knows a little about the area you're trying to learn about and ask their advice on anything you're not sure of.

Understanding That Journeys Sometimes Take a Wrong Turn

Of course, you also have to be very aware of the fact that sometimes, you can plan everything to the smallest degree but you might just end up with a problem that derails the entire thing. It's important that you allow these problems to happen and then flow away. You can also replan things once more, it's not the end just because a small problem has happened.

One of the main reasons why people don't succeed in finding their purpose and aim is that they hit a roadblock and assume that's it, it's over. They don't try and replan everything and figure things out. That basically means that the whole thing was a big waste of time.

If you want to be successful in changing your journey and moving towards your new focus, you need to be prepared for blips, and you need to have the flexibility of mind to be able to overcome them and realise that perhaps it's simply because your way wasn't the right way. That doesn't mean there isn't another way!

For instance, if you plan to buy a house and you're saving nicely, but then your car breaks down and there's no way you can do without it because you work a distance away from where you're currently living. You might think, that's it, my savings are gone, what was the point? And then you might simply avoid saving again because you stumbled at the first hurdle.

However, that is simply a blip on the road towards the success of buying your house. You don't have to give in at this point, you simply need to refocus on how you can overcome the problem.

You could perhaps commute to work for a while until you've saved up enough extra to fix the car, without dibbing into the amount you saved for your house deposit. Or, if that's counterproductive cost-wise, you could use your savings for this particular problem, understanding that it is a serious issue and not something small, and then simply pick yourself up and start again.

A small problem or an issue that comes your way doesn't have to be the end, it simply means you need to readjust your thoughts and your approach.

You could also use the same line of thinking if you were working towards changing your career. Perhaps you need to retrain and you do all the work, get your certification and you're free to start applying for jobs. You apply for several, and you're not successful. Do you give up? Some people would.

However, perhaps the better option is to ask for feedback from those interviews and work out where you can change your approach. Perhaps you're simply not answering questions in the right way, or maybe you just need to work on your confidence.

Small failures don't mean that you've completely failed, they just mean you need to readjust and think again.

Points to Take From This Chapter

This chapter has talked about the starting point you will cross when you're starting to redesign your new journey. Where you are now doesn't have to be your final destination, you simply need to work out what you want and how you're going to get it. That, however, does require some planning and research, and it also means that you need to be mindful of common pitfalls that you need to avoid.

The good news is that we've covered most of them and by reading our advice, you can do your best to sidestep the potential issues and overcome. However, of course, mistakes will happen and pitfalls will come your way; these do not mean the end, they just mean that your plan might not have been executed in the best way. You simply look at it once more and change some details.

The main points to take from this chapter are:

- Understand that knowing your purpose is the first step, and now you need to do your research in order to identify how you fulfil it and reach your final aim
- Where you are right now does not have to be your final destination, everything can and will change if you put the effort in
- There are some common pitfalls that could come your way; such as not planning well enough, not paying attention to advice, and staying within your comfort zone - you need to do your best to sidestep these
- It's completely fine to keep a few elements of your current position and incorporate them into your new journey, provided you don't simply emulate where you are and dress it up as a new journey.

Chapter 3:
The Importance of Planning

By this point, you should have an idea of what you want, and now it's time to work out how you're going to get it.

It's a good idea to write down your purpose so you can look at it on a regular basis and remind yourself of where you're working towards and what it's going to mean to you once you achieve it. The reasoning behind this is because of those common pitfalls we talked about earlier and the fact that pitfalls might come your way. When you write something down and look at it regularly, you're reiterating your desire to achieve it in your own mind and as a result, it's going to be much easier to obtain.

So, scribble it down and keep it somewhere you can see it easily. You could have it as your phone screen saver or background; you could write it on a sticky note and have it on your computer screen, or even on the bathroom mirror. The location simply needs to be somewhere you look often and where you can easily be reminded of your purpose and your desire to achieve it.

A little later on, we're going to talk about how to keep your motivation going, including using visualisation to keep that fire of desire burning hot! It's important to have that constant reminder of why you're doing something, because when you're going through a difficult time, or something does come your way which threatens to derail your journey, you can easily remind yourself of how much you want it, and as a result, you can overcome the temptation to simply give in and stay in your comfort zone.

So, let's get back to the journey at hand. We're still in the planning phase right now, and we're going to use this chapter to reiterate just how important it is to ensure your journey is carefully planned.

What Are The Elements of a Worthwhile Journey?

Whilst planning your journey, you need to be sure that it's a worthwhile route for you. Is it in line with your overall purpose? That is something you need to be sure of at the start.

It's very easy to "go off on a tangent" when you get caught up in the moment of something exciting, but it's important to stay on target and keep your mind focused. Throughout the planning process, regularly ask yourself if the journey you're planning keeps your aims in mind. Keep asking yourself if your purpose will be fulfilled by the journey you're taking.

However, we do need to make one very important point - not everything has to be planned right down to the smallest detail; you need to leave yourself some room for spontaneity!

Journeys should be vague, but they should have structure. You shouldn't plan everything right down to the smallest point and never allow yourself 'wiggle room'. What if you see an opportunity along the way which you really want to take? What if you suddenly have a desire to do a certain thing and your journey plan doesn't factor in time to try new things?

This is a very important point to make, and we're going to cover it in a bit more detail later on in this chapter when we talk about the importance of flexibility.

So, back on track - what are the elements of a journey that is truly worthwhile?

Firstly, you need to ensure that your journey is taking you where you want to go, e.g. it fulfils the purpose you have in mind. Secondly, you need to make sure that it's fun! It's no good doing something that's almost akin to 'going through the motions'! The journey has to be part of the fun, in fact, the journey should be more fulfilling than the actual final aim in many ways.

The journey also needs to teach you something, and that means you need to stretch yourself a little, perhaps push your boundaries and try things you've never done before, put yourself in positions that you've always worried about. The ironic thing is that fear is completely fake most of the time, so if you're worried about perhaps standing up in front of a room full of people and giving a presentation, that might stop you from embarking upon the nursing training you want to undertake. When you do it for the first time, however, you'll realise that you had no reason to be scared and that you're more than able to handle whatever comes your way.

Every single fear that you knock to one side will give you added confidence. You will learn things about yourself that you never understood before, and you'll achieve things you never thought you had the power to achieve. All of this makes your journey worthwhile, because who knows what you can do with those new skills and all that confidence you've developed within yourself?

So far, in our aim to identify what elements make a journey worthwhile, we have made sure that the journey is fulfilling your purpose, ensuring that the journey is fun and part of the experience, and we've talked about learning something and stretching yourself. So, what else?

Your journey needs to be flexible, because that gives you a chance to change things that might not be going well or to add in things which you might discover along the way. It also needs to be focused on the greater good.

What do we mean by that? We mean that a worthwhile journey never hurts or upsets anyone else along the way. In order for your journey to be worthwhile, it needs to be mindful of the feelings of others. If your journey tramples over someone else or upsets them in any way, how can you feel good about it when you achieve it?

In that case, your purpose is tainted and you're going to end up with pretty bad karma, assuming you believe in it.

Let's summarise. Your journey needs to be:

- Taking you towards fulfilling your purpose
- Fun
- Flexible
- It needs to teach you something and allow you to face your fears
- Not harmful or upsetting to anyone else

If the journey you're planning ticks those boxes, you're onto a good thing and you can start planning right now!

What is Important to You?

A purpose is, vaguely, something you want to work towards because it means something to you. However, not every element of your journey will be as meaningful as some of the others. This is part and parcel of life, and it's something you need to understand if you want to ensure that you don't give up simply because your journey has taken a turn for the boring. There are always ways to spruce things up!

When planning your journey, you need to ask yourself what is important to you. That means you can stay on track far easier. If something means something to you, you're more likely to stay to true to it. If something doesn't mean much to you, you're probably going to find that the temptation to throw it away and try something different, is going to be quite overwhelming.

So, whilst you're planning your journey, sit down with a pen and paper once more and write down all the things in your life and in your mind which are important to you. This light might also include things which are important to you but have not yet made an appearance in your life, perhaps the idea of having children or maybe going travelling one day. Make sure you write those down too because you need to align your purpose with all the things that are important to you, not just the things that are achievable right now. You never know what twists and turns life is going to throw at you.

Is it Time to Change Your Starting Point?

Where you are now is, as we've mentioned, not where you have to be or where you probably want to be. However, are you able to start your journey right now or do you need to wait for a little while, until the situation in your life may be better?

That's a quandary, so let's think about it for a short while.

Putting things off because the situation isn't right at the moment isn't right is both a form of procrastination and a form of sensible thinking. It really depends upon what you're doing, what your purpose is and how you want to achieve it all.

If you are currently in a very bad situation money-wise and you want to start buying a house, do you put it off until your finances are better? That's one example to think about.

Firstly, your journey can begin in several different ways, it doesn't have to be a quick out of the gates starting point. You can prepare to start without actually doing anything to damage the situation you're in now.

For instance, in this case, you could work towards minimising your money situation. If you're in debt, you could put together a payment plan to work to get rid of some of the money you owe. That could be a part of your journey and a preparation phase that gets you on the right road.

It's vital that you assess where you are now and decide whether you can do anything about the journey you want to go on at this point, or whether you need to work in a planning phase or a pre-journey phase. Don't change your ideas and plans simply because right now doesn't seem like the right time. The reason behind that is the big P - procrastination.

Another reason why you might decide now is not the right time is nothing to do with the situation you're in or any reason why it might not be a good time, and entirely to do with fear.

If you're worried about something, scared, or not sure, you're likely to put it off until a later date and tell yourself that you'll still do it, it's just that right now you need to focus on something else. The truth is that you do not need to focus on anything else, it's just that you're scared, or you have no clue where to start.

Procrastination is a serious time waster and it's something which we all fall back on when we don't want to do something, we're scared to do something, or we're not entirely sure where we should begin. In your everyday life, you probably procrastinate occasionally; we all do and it's not something to beat yourself up about if it's just an occasional habit. However, when procrastination becomes something which places barriers in the way of your success and progress in life, you need to think carefully about your reasons for delaying.

So, you need to sit down carefully and work out when is the right time to make your move and once you've pinpointed a time, you need to analyse the reason for coming to that decision. Are you making that choice because you're procrastinating or are you making that choice because it's a sensible decision? If it's the latter, make this part of your preparation phase, where you do small things to make the starting point of your journey more manageable.

By doing this, you're much more likely to succeed in reaching your aim and fulfilling your purpose.

Understanding The Need For Flexibility

We've touched upon this subject already, but it is very important and deserves a full explanation in a section of its own.

Your journey should be flexible. Remember, this is not an itinerary; you're not going to be walking around with a clipboard, ticking things off as you go. Your journey is a road you choose to travel along as part of your life, it's not a task you're going to complete as part of your time management plan!

With this in mind, you need to factor in the element of surprise, spontaneity, and flexibility. Yes, you're planning a journey and we've mentioned that you need to plan it well, but if you make it too rigid, you're simply going to rebel against it because it doesn't leave you with much else to do, or much else to enjoy. Life is for living!

When you're thinking about how long you expect your journey to last, e.g. the start and endpoint, don't be so rigid that you don't have time for fun. Make sure that this is a journey that ebbs and flows through life. If anything, however, a purpose may never have an endpoint. You may never completely fulfil your purpose because it's something which is a lifetime endeavour.

For instance, a nurse may choose to become a nurse because of a desire to help others. This is their purpose. They don't simply fulfil their purpose when they finish nursing school and obtain their first job. This is a life's calling and something which lasts until the day they hand up their nursing uniform and take some well-earned time for themselves.

It could be that your purpose is the same, or it could be that your purpose really does have an endpoint. The main thing to remember is that you don't push it to the point where you have no time for life and the things which may come your way in the meantime.

You might fall in love and get married, and that might delay your journey by a few months because you're so loved up you can't think of anything else. You might end up having children sooner than you thought, and you need to take a year or two out to enjoy their early years. Anything could happen, but that doesn't mean you need to derail your plans, it simply means you need to have the flexibility and enjoy a little spontaneity occasionally.

Your Journey Doesn't Have to Make Sense Right Now

There is another alternative we need to consider here. Maybe your journey isn't something which can be planned. Maybe it is a call, something you can do in the here and now and something which brings you a great sense of relaxation and happiness. In that case, your journey is a little different.

You might be able to reach your purpose quite quickly, but you need to maintain it. In that case, you don't need to work out how you're going to get there, e.g. your journey, but you need to organise a story instead.

There is a slight difference between the two, so let's cover those here.

- A journey is a route towards achieving something, e.g. an aim, which will allow you to either fulfil your purpose or reach it and live it out
- A story is something which you live through, e.g. a purpose which is within very easy reach and a life lived enjoying the spoils of it. That doesn't mean that you don't need to stay on track however

All of this might mean that your journey simply doesn't make sense right now, but that's fine. All you need is an idea, a starting point, and general guidance to help you get there. If you know more about it, go ahead and plan more carefully but remember the element of surprise that we talked about in our last section.

The bottom line is this - sometimes life doesn't make perfect sense. Sometimes we have no clue what we're actually doing, and we just bumble from place to place, trying to work it out. If you're living with purpose, i.e. you're fulfilling the aim you have in life and you're feeling pretty good about it, that's not a problem. It only becomes a problem when you have no clue what you want no idea how to figure it out.

Points to Take From This Chapter

In this chapter, we've talked about the importance of planning and why you need to be careful in terms of not being too rigid. Life is meant to be lived and whilst you should have an aim or a purpose in life that you're working towards or enjoying, it doesn't mean you shouldn't allow yourself opportunities to further your enjoyment in other areas.

We've also covered the fact that putting off starting your journey is only ever acceptable if you're in the middle of a pre-journey phase and not simply because you're procrastinating the life out of it, simply because you're scared.

The main points to cover are:

- Your journey needs to be a worthwhile one, and that means identifying what that means to you
- The main elements of a worthwhile journey are that the entire process is fun, you're not hurting anyone else by embarking upon it, it fulfils and works with your purpose, it is flexible, and it allows you to learn something along the way
- Your starting point might be now, or it may be slightly in the future, but you can use the current time as a pre-journey phase, a planning phase which is part of the entire process
- Putting your journey off simply because you're worried about it, you're not sure where to begin, or you're downright scared isn't a good enough excuse. This is procrastination, and it's not a good route to go down.
- Your journey needs to have space and time for flexibility and spontaneity. You cannot plan everything down to the smallest detail, and that means you need to allow yourself space to simply go with the flow to a certain degree. As long as you're not moving off course or going in a completely different direction by accident, there is no harm done
- It may not be a full journey that you need to go on, it may be more about your story. In that case, your purpose is very easy to fulfil, but it's a case of extending it and living it.

Chapter 4:
If at First You Don't Succeed

We've all heard it - if at first you don't succeed, try and try again!

That's the truth in many situations, and it's certainly the truth in this one too.

We've talked about the fact that there are likely to be roadblocks and bumps along the way and that you shouldn't give up, but it's easy to say that and not so easy to actually carry the advice through at the time. This chapter is going to address that anomaly and talk about ways you can ensure your perseverance is left unaltered by anything which causes you to veer off track slightly.

Even if you manage to fulfil your purpose, even if you can reach it quite easily and then you need to extend it, that doesn't mean the story is over. You need to realise that life is always throwing us curve balls and it's not in our power to decide if and when this happens. It just happens, and you need to develop the resilience and perseverance to overcome these challenges and move on.

The challenge may be small and, cause you a momentary lapse and slight hiccup, or it might be large and may cause you to take a pitstop for a short while, in order to overcome the problem. Whatever it is, keep your purpose in sight.

The Art of Perseverance

Perseverance is when you simply don't give up. You keep trying, you keep hacking away at something and eventually you have a breakthrough. Now, just because you persevere doesn't mean you will always get what you want, because you need to have other elements working with you too.

You need to be strong, flexible, plan well, and have a clear idea in your mind. It's no good simply having perseverance and not having the rest.

So, now we know what perseverance is, how can you develop your skills in this area?

Don't be afraid to make a mistake or fall down occasionally

Nobody is perfect, and in order to reach your aims in life, you need to cast aside the idea of perfectionism and focus on simply making progress instead. A great way to develop perseverance naturally is to embrace the moments in life which don't go your way, and the mistakes you make and learn from them. See them as a way to do better next time; a learning opportunity wrapped up as a rather questionable present.

You cannot learn to be resilient unless you experience failure occasionally, but you also need to cast aside the idea of failure being a negative thing. Yes, failure means you didn't get what you want, but it means you didn't get it that particular time; it doesn't mean you'll never get it. You also need to change your mindset and see failure as a learning curve, as we just mentioned. This mindset will serve you well through life.

Dedicate yourself to making small changes to your life every day

Perseverance can be developed by making small changes every day. By this, we mean bettering yourself at something you can already do, e.g. a skill you already possess. Aim to become a tiny bit better than you were yesterday, and you'll see that the effects turn into a huge snowball careening down a mountain; they pick up momentum with every turn.

This can also be a very motivating method too; by improving yourself, your confidence grows, and that makes you want to do even better. There is no downside when you look at it that way!

Be okay with taking small, measurable risks

In order to get by in life, you have to take small risks, and as long as those risks are healthy and you've thought them through carefully, there should be no major problem in going for it. Risks are only negative when the potential for disaster is large, or you might end up hurting yourself or someone else.

When you take risks, however, you are faced with situations and problems that you never had before. You might start to panic when this happens and pull back from the good work you've been doing, but have the bravery to stick with it. These situations allow us to become adaptable and again, help you to develop resilience.

Have a support network around you

Nobody should feel alone, and that means having a group of people around you who support you and pick you up when things get tough. This support group can act as a motivator, something to push you through when you might start to think about giving up.

When you're worried or you're facing a perseverance wall, talk to your support network, gain strength from them and keep going. These are also the ideal people to ask advice when you're not sure which way to turn.

Never forget what you're working towards

When something happens untoward, e.g. a mistake is made or something happens out of the blue, it can be easy to just throw in the towel. As we've mentioned countless times, you should view this as simply not an option. To help you with this, write down what you're trying to achieve and place it somewhere noticeable. You could also keep a copy in your bag or wallet, to look at when your will might be wavering a little.

Break your journey down into milestones

Sometimes a full journey can seem like a huge task and as a result, procrastination starts to sneak in. A great way to counteract that and build up your persistence is to break your journey, or whatever you're trying to achieve, into small and manageable milestones.

Every time you achieve a milestone, you'll feel a surge of confidence that should keep you moving on to reach the next one. Of course, you should also celebrate these with rewards, so think about going out for a meal or buying yourself something to say 'well done'.

Write down the reason 'why'

In addition to not forgetting what you're working towards, you also need to remember why. If you know why you're doing something, it's infinitely easier to keep going. Write down the reason why you're doing something and keep thinking about it and remembering it. That will motivate you on to continue and will help to build up those persistence skills we're focusing on in this section.

These elements will certainly help to boost your perseverance, and that is a huge step towards the ability to keep moving towards your purpose, aim, and anything else you want in life.

Does Your Journey Need to be Altered Slightly?

It could be that you need to change your journey just a little. This realisation might come at the beginning of the process, whilst you're trying to plan everything out, or it might come part-way through when you realise that something might just not be working out too well.

There is a very big difference between giving up because you've been knocked off track or your motivation has left you, and altering your journey a little because you've realised something isn't working.

If you need to make changes, understand that you've not failed or done anything wrong, you've simply realised that the route isn't going to work as it is. In many ways, seeing this at this point is actually a positive element; it means you're determined to make it work.

Changes can be a good thing because it can be the kick you need to get things moving again. If you were stuck before, perhaps you found yourself static, and things just weren't working out and you couldn't understand the reason why, changing your approach slightly might be all you need to get things moving once more.

So, if you do hit a plateau if you notice that things aren't really going the way you thought, first think about your expectations and whether they're truly manageable or not. It could be that you had completely unrealistic expectations and the reason why nothing is going as you wanted it to is that you overstretched yourself. In that case, think carefully about what is realistic and what isn't.

If that isn't the case, it could also be that a few tweaks need to be made here and there. That doesn't mean you need to go back to the drawing board, but it might mean you need to make a few subtle alterations to start things going the way you want them to once more.

How to Build Motivation to Keep Moving Forwards

Perseverance and motivation are very closely linked, but they're not exactly the same.

Motivation is the will to do something, a drive if you will, but persistence is the ability to stay on course, even if something stands in your way. To simplify, motivation is what kickstarts you and pushes you on, whilst persistence keeps you on track.

In order to be successful, you need both motivation and perseverance in place, as one will feed off the other.

It can be hard to remain motivated when small things come your way. For instance, you might have been through a period of illness and it's left you feeling a little tired and lethargic. That lack of desire to do whatever it is you're aiming towards could easily cause you to just not bother, and as a result of your will to continue just fades and disappears for good. However, there are many ways to keep your motivation levels high and to regain motivation when it seems to have upped sticks and ran away for a while.

So, how can you increase your motivation, allowing you to stay on course and work hand in hand with your persistence?

Remember Your Why

Do you remember in our last section on persistence we talked about needing to know your "why" in order to overcome problems? The same goes for your motivation in many ways. The thing is, motivation is often the will to get started, whilst persistence keeps you going.

If you know why you're doing something, it's much easier to get started on it and keep going with it. You can then keep reminding yourself of your reason why when you're struggling or when things might be starting to feel a little too difficult for you to handle.

In many ways, your why is your purpose, and keeping that at the forefront of your mind, perhaps writing it down, will help you in a big way.

Avoid Analysing Too Much

Are you guilty of overthinking? Most of us are, but the problem with overthinking is that it doesn't really do anything useful. All overthinking does is robs us of the joy we're feeling in the here and now and actually reduces your motivation because you're terrified about the worst-case scenario you've dreamed up and the chances of it becoming true.

Keep things as simple as possible and just keep moving forward, even if the pace at which you're moving isn't as fast as you would like it to be.

If you're someone who regularly struggles with anxiety, you'll probably find that you're a natural over-thinker, but you need to start challenging these thoughts and asking yourself why you're trying to sabotage your own efforts. However, we'll cover the damaging effects of negative self-talk and how to fix it in a later chapter.

Break The Journey Down

Again, you need to break your journey down into smaller segments which are easier to manage and you need to celebrate every success along the way. If you find that procrastination is a real problem for you, how about using delayed gratification as a tactic to push yourself on?

This basically means that you promise yourself a specific treat if you manage to achieve a specific task. You might decide to book yourself a weekend away when you've reached a specific milestone in your journey. E.g. if you're saving up for a house you might decide to have a holiday and a slight break from saving when you reach the halfway point of your target savings amount.

Not everyone is a fan of delayed gratification, but there's no denying that it certainly works. It's something you can try for yourself and see what you respond best to.

Many of the methods to boost your motivation are very similar to boosting your perseverance, but the key is to understanding that getting started is usually the hardest part. Once you've taken a step forward and you're on your way, the effects of momentum tend to take over. As a result, you're moving with every item you tick off your list, even if you're moving slowly, or you suddenly pick up speed and tick several items off your list very quickly.

The speed at which you move doesn't really matter when it comes to achieving your purpose. There is no race here, and you're not trying to compete with anyone else. If that's your aim, you need to sit down and really think about why you're on this path in the first place.

A purpose is something that is important to you and you alone. It's not about impressing someone or trying to keep up with someone. Everyone has their own path to follow, their own purpose and their own list of things they want to achieve in life. You can't copy anyone else's, and they can't copy yours; if you do this, or they do this, nobody is going to be fulfilled and there's going to be a whole group of people who thought they were doing the right thing but find themselves living with regrets in the future.

For that reason, you need to be strong in your will and your desire to reach your purpose in life. You cannot expect success if you don't have those things. If you know what you want and why, however, and you know that you're doing it for yourself and nobody else, there's a very strong chance that with a dose of persistence and plenty of motivation, you'll get to where you want to be.

Change Your View of Who You Are

When you're not happy with your position in life, it's hard to really like who you are.

Do you agree?

You might feel like you're missing something, a piece of you has gone astray, and you might feel like you're just not whole or complete. You might feel unhappy too, which could easily lead you towards coping mechanisms which simply aren't healthy, such as drinking, smoking, or overeating.

When you're not happy with your life, it's hard to be upbeat and positive about much. You simply settle for what you have, and you think that being 'just okay' is how you're supposed to be. The problem is, being 'just okay' doesn't lend itself to lifelong happiness and it doesn't give you the strength or will to overcome problems that life might throw your way.

As part of your journey, and especially at the start, you need to change your view of who you are right now.

Let's grab that pen and paper again and do a spot of brainstorming.

Who do you think you are? Are you a strong person? Are you motivated? Are you caring? Kind? Honest? What are your strengths and what are your weaknesses? Write them all down. It doesn't matter if the piece of paper looks like a scribbled mess at this point, it's just important to get the information out of your mind and onto a page, so you can organise it later.

Looking at the paper, does your purpose align with your strengths and what weaknesses can you work to improve? What kind of person does that make you right now?

Identify something you want to change and work towards changing it, but make sure you don't overload yourself and you only stick with one or two elements at a time. By making small steps to becoming the person you want to be, you'll make progress.

It's likely that the journey you want to embark upon, and the journey you're going to embark upon, is going to change you somewhat. Any type of self-development journey or item has the habit of changing certain elements of your personality, but it's all for the better.

For instance, someone who has been on a weight loss journey may find that they become a more confident person, and they develop a more positive mindset and attitude towards food. They might also start to realise that people look at them and treat them differently now they're slimmer and start to resent the fact that maybe they didn't get the same attention or respect before.

A person who has quit their job and retrained in a totally different field may find that they're also more confident but that they're more resilient too. They may find that they're able to overcome difficulties more easily, when before they might have looked at everything with a negative viewpoint.

Everything you encounter in your life leaves its mark on you in some way, and when you're embarking on a journey that is literally going to help you fulfil a purpose and improve your current place, changes are certainly going to happen.

Do not try and resist these changes because they're part and parcel of the journey. These changes are necessary in order for you to make progress. Without going through a few changes you're just going to stay where you are, and that's not going to help you work towards your purpose or feel fulfilled.

The only thing you need to be careful of is to be mindful that any changes you notice in yourself are positive ones only. Avoid becoming overconfident and perhaps arrogant due to your happiness at working towards what you want. Remain humble and remember that all of this is coming your way because of hard work and persistence, but also because others around you are probably helping you too.

We should also talk about the way you view yourself right now.

The reason is that most of us don't see ourselves in the same way that others do. This can be for a whole host of reasons, but it's normal down to a lack of confidence or past experiences that have planted a seed of negativity in our minds and told us that we couldn't do something, or we're not good enough.

Earlier in the book, we talked about societal expectations and cultural ones too. These can often form a view in your mind of who you are, but how do you know if that view is accurate or not? If society tells you to do something, you need to be sure that it's in alignment with what you want before you go ahead with it. The same goes for any cultural expectations that are placed upon you.

Sure, cultural expectations are very difficult to manage, especially if you live or come from an area that has very strong expectations for gender, etc. In some cultures, the woman is expected to stay home and look after the home and the children, and she's not expected to go out and work, carve out a career or even have an education. Many women in that kind of situation don't even think about changing where they are because it's become so ingrained in their psyche of what they're 'supposed' to do that they don't even think about making alterations to their point.

In that type of situation, if that woman is happy and fulfilled and if she feels that she's working towards, or she's hit her purpose, then there is no work to do. However, what if she feels unfulfilled, what if she's seen a magazine from another culture which talks about how women are out there and going to university, training for high flying jobs? She might start to resent where she is and want to make changes, but find herself tied to her culture too tightly.

That's a gender example, but the same goes for any gender; there are cultural and societal examples such as this we could talk about all day long. The point is, staying in line with your culture or what society expects when you're truly not happy, and you're dreaming of something different, is not going to fulfil you. You're not living the life you want or need and you don't have an accurate view of who you really are.

In that case, perhaps you need to sit down and do some very deep thinking about who you are, what you stand for, what is important to you deep down and how important your culture or the wishes of society are to you too. Only when you embrace your needs, wants and desires can you make any changes of note, and only then can you view yourself in the way in which you're supposed to be seen.

The bottom line is that you can do anything you set your mind to, within reason. Yes, there are barriers and limitations for many people, but these aren't always totally impossible. It's time to realise who you are and what you want and work towards making it a reality, rather than trying to please everyone else all the time. If you dedicate your life to being a people pleaser and saying "yes" constantly, you're never going to be happy or fulfilled, and your purpose will simply pass you by.

Points to Take From This Chapter

This chapter has talked at length about how to keep going when things might come your way and attempt to derail you. We've talked about motivation, perseverance, we've talked about looking at who you are and perhaps changing your view of yourself, and we've talked about cultural and societal expectations that can often hold us back.

Sometimes your journey may need to change course a little or just be altered slightly. That's fine, don't worry about it, and don't use it as an excuse to give up!

The main points to take from this chapter are:

- In order to get started with anything in life you need motivation
- Perseverance and motivation are two different things; motivation gets you started and keeps you going, and perseverance helps you overcome barriers that might seek to hold you back
- Your journey may need to change course slightly, but that isn't a reason to allow yourself to be derailed completely or give up
- Motivation can be increased, as can perseverance, but you need to learn how to do this and dedicate yourself to the cause

- You might need to look at your current view of yourself and work out whether it is accurate in order to find the strength to keep moving in your journey
- There are many societal and cultural expectations that are placed on people, and these can often shape their view of who they are, to the point where they really miss out on the things that they dream of doing. It's fine to break free from these and focus on yourself
- Your journey is going to change you in some ways, but that's fine as long as the changes are positive.

Chapter 5:
The Power of Your Own Mind

The most powerful thing you own is sitting in your head.

Think about that for a second.

Yes, we are talking about your brain, your mind, whatever you want to call it

Scientists are still trying to figure out the capacity of the human brain and what it is capable of. It seems that it is capable of so much that it's taking years and years and years of research! That can only be a good thing for you because it means you can tap into the power of your mind and use it to overcome problems, keep going when things get tough, and find the confidence and will to make changes that you need in order to get to where you want to be in life.

In this chapter, we're going to talk about the things you can do, placed solely in your mind, to keep you moving towards what you want and what you need in life. These strategies and ideas will help you to avoid giving up and will put you on the path towards success.

It seems that every single day there is something negative to focus on, but there are a million positives out there if you take the time to look. Changing your mindset from negative to positive is the first thing you should focus on doing, and that's something we're going to talk about at length very shortly. However, before you get to that point, you need to accept and acknowledge the reality of the situation - you are capable of far more than you currently think, and all you need to do is tap into the power of your own mind in order to be able to use the tools you already have at your disposal.

We're not going to go down the "anything is possible" route here, because in reality not every single thing you can dream of in life is possible; however, most things are if you plan the route out carefully and use the power of your mind to overcome obstacles.

You have more problem-solving skills than you realise. You have more confidence inside of you than you might now. You're capable of far more than you have achieved so far. You simply need to believe it and then develop an unwavering desire to get to where you want to be.

So, let's start with your mindset first and foremost.

Kicking Out Negative Self-Talk

The human brain is hard-wired to be negative first and positive second. That's just the way we are developed and it all stems back to the days when cavemen and women were wandering the Earth, trying to avoid being eaten by huge predators.

At that time, danger was literally around every corner, and in order to cope with that type of lifestyle, the human brain adapted itself. The strategy it used was, and still is, called "fight or flight".

This is the stress response that occurs within the body whenever the human brain perceives what it thinks is a treat. The problem is, most of the time it gets it wrong. We don't have the same number of threats to face as the cavemen and women had, in fact, we hardly have any compared to them. It's simply that the human brain hasn't quite caught up with that yet and it's still stuck in 'looking out for danger' mode.

Of course, this is designed to keep you safe. When the brain is constantly scanning your environment for threats, it's looking to kickstart the stress response whenever it sees something which really could actually be a threat at some point. When this threat is seen, the response is activated; your brain releases hormones and endorphins to help you cope with it, allowing your body to either fight the threat, or run away from it.

The issue? Most threats the brain perceives don't need to be run away from or fought, they simply need to be managed. In fact, sometimes the perceived threat isn't a threat of any kind at all, and the brain has got it all wrong.

This can easily leave you in a constant state of stress and awareness. Over time, being switched on to such a degree can be very detrimental, and it can cause you to be so overwhelmed that doing anything is a huge struggle.

Stress isn't something to take lightly, in fact over time, when prolonged and severe, stress can be a killer.

So, how does a negative mindset tie into this?

We're hardwired to be negative first and foremost because it makes us pessimistic and pessimism is thought to make us look for dangers in things that are dressed up as positive items. This is the brain's way of scanning the environment for danger.

However, it's entirely possible to change your default setting from negative to positive, and this will certainly help you achieve your aims and work towards your purpose.

How?

Because positive thinking pushes you forwards. It gives you hope and in many cases also helps with your general health and wellbeing.

When you're positive, you're healthier, you have more energy, you're always on the lookout for opportunities, and you're more likely to take them because your newfound confidence tells you that you can.

We should point out that changing a negative mindset into a positive one isn't always easy and does take time. The best way to go about this is through a process called 'reframing'.

Reframing is a popular cognitive behavioural therapy technique (CBT) which is used in several different situations; becoming more positive is just one of them. The problem is, reframing takes time, and it's quite tiring at first because it means you need to be mindful of every single thought you have and you need to figure out quickly whether what you're thinking is positive or negative. The chances are that at this point you're having more negative thoughts than positive ones, but you should work with just one thought at a time, to avoid overwhelming yourself and stressing yourself out.

Try this.

- Be mindful of your thoughts and the next time you identify that you're having a negative thought, accept it. Say to yourself "I am experiencing a thought which is negative". By doing this, you're telling yourself that this thought needs to be changed because it's not in line with your aims of becoming more positive.
- Examine the thought and come up with an alternative. For example, if the thought you had is "I am so tired of working all the time", you need to reframe that thought into something more positive. It can be anything, but it needs to resonate with you. Perhaps you could reframe that thought to "I am working hard to fund my dreams", or "I am working hard to afford a holiday". You basically need to take the negative thought and turn it into something far more positive.
- When you've come up with something that sits well with you, you need to repeat it. Repetition is key here. We learn by repetition; do you remember when you were a child at school, and the teacher kept making you sing the colours of the rainbow in a song over and over again? They did this because repetition helps your brain to remember things, by forming new connections.

- Repeat the new positive thought a few times whilst thinking about the problem at hand. You can either say it aloud or you can say it in your mind, whatever works for you. Keep repeating it whenever the thought comes up.
- Over time, the new positive thought will replace the negative one, and when you think about work in the future, you're more likely to think about the holiday you're saving up for as a result of work, than the fact that you're tired of it.

It's best to work with one thought at a time and not try and reframe too many in one go. Reframing might sound simple but in practice, it's quite heavy. You need to really dedicate to changing the thought into a positive in order for it to work and if you don't do this, the negative is simply going to stick and breakthrough whenever you try and change it.

Once one thought has stuck, work with another, and so on until you notice that you're naturally starting to have more positive thoughts overall.

There is no timescale of how long this will take; everyone is different and it depends upon the degree to which you're positive or negative already. However, over a period of time of reframing thoughts, your brain will start to rewire itself, and you'll notice yourself becoming a more positive person.

All of this helps you to deal with problems and issues that come your way, and help you to become more motivated too. With all of this working together, you'll notice that your new journey and your purpose are within easier reach than if you'd stuck with the old negative model.

Of course, positivity also helps you to become a happier, healthier and more centred kind of person. Everyone wants to be around the happy and positive types of people, and as a result, you're probably going to notice that your social circle widens and you develop stronger relationships as a result.

There are no downsides when it comes to developing a positive mindset, it's simply going to take time to actually stick.

Becoming more positive is also easier if you dedicate yourself to looking after number one too. That means eating a healthy diet, exercising on a regular basis, getting plenty of sleep, and talking about any problems that are bothering you. When you focus on yourself, you're investing in yourself too - there is no better investment than that!

Be Kind to Yourself

Do you regularly talk to yourself in your mind? Most of us do, so don't worry; you're not going insane!

When you talk to yourself and tell yourself to do things or not do things, is the voice in your head negative? Are you quite tough on yourself?

It's likely to be that way.

Most of us are very tough on ourselves and easier on those around us. Why is it okay to speak to your friends and family with compassion and love, but you speak to yourself with nothing but chagrin and annoyance? Why don't you deserve the same kind of love and attention that you give to everyone else, but not yourself?

That's a question that has long puzzled the world.

You need to be more kind to yourself in order to develop the strength to keep moving on when things come your way and to get you started in the first place.

Perhaps you tell yourself automatically that you can't do something. Perhaps you're pulling yourself down all the time but bigging everyone else up. It's a common trait, but it's one which needs to stop if you want to make any kind of headway in your journey towards fulfilling your purpose.

In many ways, learning to love yourself is part of your purpose too!

We're going to talk about self-compassion a little more shortly, but for now, you also need to know that being kind to yourself covers your health and wellbeing.

You need to aim for at least 7-8 hours of sleep every single day, and you shouldn't place sleep at the bottom of your importance list. How can you do anything if you're tired? How are you supposed to feel motivated and find the strength to overcome problems if you're lacking energy and your eyes just want to close so you can nod off to sleep?

In addition, you need to eat that varied diet we mentioned before, packed with vitamins and minerals to give you all the nutrition you need for optimum health and wellbeing.

You also need to focus on exercise.

Many people hear the word 'exercise' and automatically think about gyms, sweat, and general unpleasantness, but exercise does not have to be that way, in fact, it shouldn't be that way!

Find a form of exercise that you like and enjoy and do more of it. That's really how simple it is. It could be running, walking, jogging, Zumba, a team sport, exercise classes, swimming, yoga, or even the gym. Whatever you want and enjoy, you can do in order to boost your health and wellbeing.

You might be wondering how this is going to help you achieve your purpose and work towards your aims in life, but it all comes down to health and wellbeing once more.

When you're healthier, you're more able to think carefully and make decisions. You're also more likely to be able to consider risks in a better way, and you're going to avoid unhealthy coping mechanisms too.

The opposite is true when you don't dedicate enough time to health and wellbeing.

You'll be tired, lacking in energy, your immune system may be low, and you'll start picking up all manner of viruses, and it all boils down to a rather negative picture which does nothing to help you achieve your aims in life.

Of course, being kind to yourself and doing the things you love occasionally is no bad thing anyway. It helps you to become more relaxed, less stressed out, and it gives you the power to understand your own importance. You cannot be the best version of yourself if you don't look after yourself enough to get there!

Create Solid Habits to Push You Forwards

One way to ensure that you stay on track with anything in life is to create a series of habits that work to push you forwards and support your aims.

You probably already have several habits in your life, but you need to ask yourself whether they're useful or helpful, or whether they're actually hindering your progress. For instance, procrastination can become a habit, and that's a very damaging one to have in your life. Equally, having lay-ins at the weekend and sleeping late is also a very dangerous habit, because it completely messes up your body clock and causes you to be tired and sluggish for the following couple of days.

It's important that you realise that there are healthy and unhealthy habits, and much of the time we don't even realise when we're doing something unhealthy because it seems to be so easy and part of our daily lives. It's that way because you've repeated it that many times that it's now second nature.

If you define a habit, you'll come up with something like a routine or practice that you repeat and find hard to give up. Habits can't just be thrown out of the window because you have decided they're not for you, they take time and work to try and get away from. In the same way, setting new habits also take time to establish and become part of your daily routine and therefore become a habit.

Do you have many unhealthy habits? Think carefully and write them down. A few examples of unhealthy habits include:

- Smoking
- Drinking too much at the weekends, or when you feel that you're stressed
- Overeating to deal with stress or upset
- Not having a regular sleeping pattern in place, e.g. sleeping longer at the weekends
- Exercising too much as a distraction to your problems
- Procrastination

How many of those habits can you nod your head too? It's possible that you have many more. It's not something to be ashamed of, but it is something you need to be honest about and realise that it needs to change. Once you start making steps to change something, you'll realise that it's not as hard as you thought.

You might wonder how this helps you with your journey and your purpose, but having strong and healthy habits help to keep you on track and allow you to be more centred and grounded in your life. They also help you to deal with problems and stress in a healthy way, rather than allowing it to throw you off track and cause your emotions to spike and rise. You can rely upon your healthy habits rather than your negative ones in that case.

A good way to do this is to take one negative habit at a time and replace it with something positive. Don't try and change more than one at a time as you'll find it overwhelming. Remember, a habit it something ingrained and long-standing, so it's not going to change overnight. However, with a little time and persistence, you'll notice that changes come your way.

Choose a habit, one which you feel has the most impact on you first. Identify it and acknowledge that it is negative. In order to do this, you have to realise why that is. Why is it negative and what impact does it have on you?

For instance, let's take laying in at the weekend as our example here. You might think at first that there's nothing wrong with having a little extra sleep at the weekend when you've worked hard all week, but it's negative because you need to have a regular sleeping cycle in order to be healthy and stay alert. When you don't do this, you throw your body clock into chaos and you start to feel agitated and unfocused. Procrastination is far easier when you feel this way.

So, the first step here is to understand why sleeping in late at the weekend is damaging. Once you've done that, look at ways you can replace that bad habit with one which is far more healthy. In this case, you could say that you're going to set your alarm to the same time every day and you're going to get up and make the most of the extra hours you have to do whatever you want at the weekend.

If you normally get up at 8am in the week, make sure you get up at 8am at the weekend too. Before you roll your eyes and wonder why that is supposed to make you happy, wait for a second! You don't have to go to work, so you can spend the extra time in the morning making a delicious breakfast, lounging on the sofa with a coffee in hand, you can spend a little 'me' time relaxing. You're still ensuring that your body clock is where it should be, but you're also giving yourself a different kind of weekend treat, one which is a little healthier and aimed at self-care.

Then, you need to actually do it. It might be difficult the first time you do it, but it will get easier. Keep at it and you'll find that eventually, you'll set a new habit that is far more positive than the old one. However, if you find that you feel yourself slipping back into the old habit, be sure to pull yourself back and remind yourself of the reason why you're changing it, and the reason why it is negative.

Another example is smoking. It's very hard to give up smoking, this is something we need to acknowledge, so this isn't a habit you can instantly change and work to repeat, like the one we just mentioned. However, this habit needs to be done in baby steps, with total and firm determination.

Again, identify why smoking is a bad habit. It is bad because it is damaging to your health and you use it as a crutch during stressful times. If you need to, do some online research into the harmful effects of smoking, to really solidify your reasoning.

Once you've done that, work out the best way to quit. You might need to go and see your doctor to work out a smoking cessation programme, and if that's the case, that's fine, do it. It might not have to be your doctor, you might be able to go and see your local pharmacist, but do whatever feels right to you. Identify the best way to quit for you; this might be nicotine patches, it might be cutting down and then stopping, or it might be going cold turkey. Nobody can tell you what to do here, you have to choose your right option, but you need to ensure that you keep the reason you're changing this unhealthy habit clear in your mind.

Then, you need to change your unhealthy habit (smoking) and replace it with a positive one. Why not take up a sport or a type of exercise that you enjoy? That means you're replacing a habit that is bad for your health with one which is good for your health. Again, repetition is key, so keep at it and keep reminding yourself why you're doing it. With time and perseverance, you'll get there and you'll feel wonderful because of it. This in itself is likely to catapult you towards the success you want in terms of reaching your purpose and your aims in life. It's possible to find confidence everywhere if you look hard enough!

Once you've changed one habit, make sure that it's solidified before you start trying to change another. Just because you've replaced one and repeated the new habit a few times, doesn't mean that it's going to be sticking forever. You might have the odd 'fall off the wagon' and in that case you need to stick with it until you feel like you've totally replaced it. Then, you can choose another and use the same process to change that one.

Eventually, you will find that you change several habits and replace them with healthy ones. However, nobody is ever without at least one or two bad habits. We're human after all and that means that occasionally you're going to do something a few times over which becomes ingrained. As long as this isn't detrimental to your health, it's not detrimental to anyone else, and it's not affecting your purpose, you can work to replace that at some point in the future. Don't try and be perfect, simply do your best.

The Power of Affirmations And Visualisation

Throughout this chapter, we're talking about ways to effectively re-wire your brain and become more focused on what you're aiming towards. Another very effective way, or two effective ways, to continue with this is to use affirmations and visualisation techniques.

Let's talk about each one in turn, with affirmations first of all.

Earlier in this chapter, we talked about the power of

positivity and how you can change a default negative setting into a positive one. We used the art of reframing in that situation, but we also need to talk about affirmations too.

Affirmations can be used in several different situations, including changing your mindset from negative to positive and also to help you achieve something and stay on track.

An affirmation is a statement of intent, words you choose which sum up your mindset and what you want to achieve, and which are then repeated over and over until they become stuck in your mind and your brain believes them to be true.

Again, the key here is repetition.

Let's use weight loss as an example here.

Perhaps your purpose is to live a healthy life, using vegan food and mindfulness techniques. However, at the moment, you need to become healthier and lose some weight, and you actually have quite a lot of weight to lose in order to reach your first aim.

No problem, it's totally doable, although of course not easy.

If this is your purpose, you will have created a journey to get you there, and from that point, you will continue to live your life in a way which honours vegan practices and the mindfulness techniques you want to use. However, losing the weight is something you're struggling with because cravings keep trying to knock you off track.

In this case, you need to come up with an affirmation that reminds you of your power and why you're trying to lose weight. When a craving comes your way, and you're on the brink of reaching for something unhealthy and undoing your good work for the day, you would then repeat your affirmation a few times and pull your mind back to the mindset you want it to be at.

Your affirmation needs to be personal to you, and the words need to resonate with who you are and what you believe. You cannot simply copy someone else's affirmation because it won't be as personal and therefore won't work. You'll just pass it off as words and you'll end up giving in. However, if you do some research into potential affirmations and then add your own personal twist, this could be a good way for you.

A few suggestions are:

- "I am strong; I will not give in"
- "I have the power to change my weight"
- "I will not succumb to temptation; I am stronger than temptation"
- "The fate of my health is in my hands"

It can be anything, but you get the idea.

Once you've created your affirmation, spend a little time really feeling it. This means assessing whether or not it's the right one for you. Do you feel something when you read it? Does it light a fire inside of you and make you want to take action? That's a sign of a good affirmation.

The next step is to write it down and keep it somewhere visible and easily accessible. This could be on a sticky note on your computer screen, on your bathroom mirror, on the refrigerator door, or as an alert on your phone which pops up every few hours.

When you wake up in the morning, close your eyes and repeat the affirmation three or four times. Say it aloud if you can, but if that's not possible you can say the words in your head. You need to really tune into the words in order for them to be powerful, so make sure you give them your full attention and don't just say them for saying's sake.

Repeat this again at lunchtime, again in the evening and again before you go to bed. If you feel yourself wobbling, e.g. you're about to give in to temptation, say it again in order to pull your mind back to the right point.

Over time you'll find that your affirmation becomes second nature and you don't have to look at a piece of paper in order to remember it. It becomes part of who you are and your entire belief system.

Affirmations are extremely powerful but they hinge on how you believe in them. If you see them as nothing more than mumbo-jumbo, they're just not going to work for you. However, give them a go first and see how they work for you before you make a judgement. Many mindfulness techniques are passed off as nothing more than hippy rubbish, but over time people start to try them and realise that there is something very positive to be found within them. These techniques have not stuck around for this long for no reason at all!

You can create an affirmation for anything at all and they can be very motivating. If you simply want to become a more positive person, you can use an affirmation such as "I am positive and happy". If you want to become more motivated, you could use an affirmation such as "I will not give up, I am determined".

Whatever works for you is the route you should continue with.

Next up, let's talk about visualisation.

You can use visualisation alongside affirmations with great effect; however, they can also be used as a standalone technique too. Perhaps you don't find the greatest joy with affirmations, but you're able to connect to visualisations far more easily. The opposite could also be true. We're all individuals, so go with what helps you stay on track.

Visualisation exercises are about imagining how something is going to look when it is complete. By doing this, you get to almost touch and feel the experience. The idea here is that by having almost experienced it before, you can pull that memory to the front of your mind and use it as a motivator to continue onwards when you're struggling or when you simply need a boost of 'get up and go'.

Visualisation isn't a meditation technique per se, but it is used in meditation, so if you've ever tried meditation, you might already have a head start on this one. The problem is, many people struggle with visualisation because it means you need to block out the noise from outside and really concentrate on what you're trying to picture in your mind. This does get easier over time, so the key here is to keep trying and don't be discouraged if you don't succeed the first few times. You will get there in the end.

Let's look at an example. Perhaps your purpose and journey is about travel. You want to experience the world and see new things, have new experiences, but you are stuck at the moment because you have debt and you need to start saving up.

Your journey, in this case, will be about minimising your debt and then eventually getting rid of it, whilst saving up enough money to start travelling. This will be a long road, but in order to stay on track, you can use visualisation.

Try this:

- Find somewhere comfortable and either sit or lay down. Make sure you're warm enough and that nothing is going to distract you from the visualisation technique you're about to do. If you feel like someone is going to walk in and disturb you, try and find a more suitable time. You should also turn your phone onto silent or turn it off completely.
- Close your eyes and focus on your breath. Notice your chest rising and falling with each inhalation and exhalation.
- Breathe in through your nose for a count of five in a slow and controlled manner. Hold the breath for a count of three and then exhale through your mouth in the same controlled manner as before. Repeat this

until you feel relaxed and your mind has slowed and quietened.
- When you're ready, start to picture the thing you're trying to work towards, e.g. your purpose. In this case, you need to imagine that you are on that travel journey and you're seeing the world. Try and picture this in as much detail as possible, so choose one destination that you want to see the most.
- Notice the small details, such as the sun on your skin, the smell in the air, the light glistening off the walls, and the small details of the destination as much as you can.
- Try and tune in to how you feel when you're in this destination. Do you feel happy? Content? Full of wonder? Try and really feel the emotions that the place is causing you to feel and commit them to memory.
- Spend some time in the visualisation to really commit the whole thing to your memory. The idea is that you can recall the details of the visualisation whenever you need a boost of motivation or when your will might be wavering.
- Don't spend more than a few minutes in the visualisation at first as you will become exhausted. When you're ready, tell yourself that you're going to return to the room now and slowly open your eyes.

Visualisations such as this are quite powerful because you can almost feel the emotions associated with being in the place. You should try and repeat the exercise several times, so perhaps once every couple of days, in order to really get it into your mind. After that, you can simply call upon it when you need to.

Using this example, if you feel that things are starting to waver, e.g. you're struggling with saving and you simply want to go out and spend some cash, remind yourself of your aim and your new journey by pulling the visualisation to your mind. You'll notice that you start to feel the same emotions as when you were deep in the exercise and that should be enough to stop you from acting upon the temptation you're experiencing.
You can alternate between affirmations and visualisations if you want to, or you can simply use just one. See which works best for you and go with that. However, the key in both of these techniques is belief.

You have to believe that they're going to work; otherwise it's simply a waste of time. If at first, your belief is a little shaky, keep on trying. You will probably find that the more you try it, the more you believe in it, and the more you can use it to help keep you on track when your resolve might be wavering a little.

You see, the reason is this - there is no journey on the planet which is without its problems, without its pitfalls, and without its challenges. Even the seemingly simplest to journeys is going to have its issues occasionally but you can get through them provided you have the right mindset. Using the techniques we've talked about in this chapter will give you the tools to overcome those issues and keep going towards your purpose in life.

Why Self Compassion Needs to be a Part of Your Journey

Be honest, do you find it hard to put yourself first?

Most of us do and it's because we're somehow told that focusing on ourselves means we're being selfish.

The truth is that there is nothing selfish about self-care and self-compassion, and these are elements of a healthy life. If you constantly place attention and effort on others and never think about yourself occasionally, how are you supposed to be happy and healthy?

Do you always say "yes" when you don't have the time to do something? Are you always running around doing things for other people and never really getting the time to do the things you want to do?

These are common problems in the modern-day and it's something which has to change.

You're not selfish for saying "no" to a request that you just don't have the time for. You're not selfish for spending a little time and home recharging your batteries rather than joining your friend for the drinks they invited you out for. It's totally fine to take a day off and do nothing other than pampering yourself. These are necessary things.

Self-compassion basically means that you're easy on yourself. If you're constantly pulling yourself down, as we mentioned earlier when we talked about negative self-talk, you're never going to believe in your own power, and you're going to fall at every hurdle.

Be kind to yourself, and that means looking after number one occasionally. It means forgiving yourself if you give in to temptation just once and not beating yourself up internally for being human. We all falter sometimes, you can't be expected to be perfect!

Of course, we do try to be perfect, because society tells us we have to be. The thing is, what is perfect anyway? Is there an actual reference point of what perfectionism is? What does it look like? What does it taste like? What does it feel like?

Everyone has a different opinion on what perfect is, so how are you supposed to reach that ideal when everyone has a different idea of what it is? It's impossible and you'll run yourself into the ground attempting to do it.

It's a far better idea to simply be yourself and focus on that. Go for what you want and be kind to yourself and others. Whilst you should certainly not trample over anyone else to reach what you want, you shouldn't feel that you have you to hold yourself back for everyone either. If someone accuses you of being too focused on your aim, take it as a compliment. If someone complains that they don't get to see you as much as they used to, do your best to see them a little more, but don't let it distract you from what you want to achieve.

This is your journey, your story, and your life. If you're always telling others how it's okay to do something wrong occasionally and giving them advice on being positive, telling them how great they are, why aren't you doing the same for yourself?

We often give great advice for others but when it comes to ourselves, we're clueless and we'd much rather drag ourselves down and berate ourselves for one small error than shrug our shoulders and say "ah well, I'll learn from it next time". Because that's what you have to do whenever you make a mistake or fall a little, you have to pick yourself up and figure out how you can learn from it. How can you avoid it happening again, or what have you learnt as a result of that mistake?

It's a far better mindset to have than simply ripping yourself own constantly and telling yourself that you're not good enough. You are more than good enough.

Points to Take From This Chapter

This chapter has been all about how to strengthen your mindset and work towards achieving what you want in life. The strategies we've mentioned are ideal for overcoming struggles and challenges and can help to push you towards your aims and desires in life as a result. They're also strategies you can call upon when you're struggling with motivation and determination and can strengthen your sense of persistence in the process.

It's important to point out that your journey is not going to be perfect and you should not expect it to be. Just because a small mistake happens or something doesn't go quite according to plan, that doesn't mean everything is ruined and completely over. It just means that you need to brush yourself up and carry on. We all make mistakes occasionally, it's part and parcel of being human; you simply need to make sure that it doesn't stop you from carrying on and doesn't cause your self-confidence to dip as a result.

The main points to take from this chapter are:

- A positive mindset will help you overcome many things in life but you will need to do some work in order to change your default setting from negative to positive
- Reframing negative thoughts into positive ones is a great way to develop a more positive mindset
- Affirmations are a good strategy for helping to keep you on track but can also be used when changing to a more positive way of thinking
- Affirmations need to be personal to you, so you need to spend some time really thinking about what works for you
- Visualisation techniques allow you to almost feel the thing you're working towards before you've got this. This will push you on to succeed, because you can call upon the memory whenever you might be struggling
- Visualisation takes time and effort and effort. You might not get it right the first time, but you should persevere and keep going
- Mistakes happen in life and you need to accept that you will make them occasionally. You need to see mistakes as learning curves and not reasons to give up or reasons to talk to yourself in a negative way
- Perfection doesn't exist so it's pointless trying to achieve it

- We all put others in front of our own wellbeing, but self-compassion has to be part of your journey if you want to live a healthy and happy life
- It is okay to say "no" to things you don't want to do, or things you haven't got the time for.

Chapter 6:
What Comes Next?

We've talked a huge amount so far about why achieving your purpose is something which is in reach, provide you put in the time and effort. We've also talked a lot about how to stay on track and how to keep going towards your purpose when perhaps life seems to be throwing you curve balls at every opportunity.

By this point, the hope is that you know whether or not this is a journey you need to embark upon. If you're not happy with your life, the only thing you can do is change it. Otherwise, your story will never change, and you will continually live in a way that doesn't fulfil you and doesn't make you happy. The effects of that can be very damaging over time and will cause you to regret all the things you wanted, but never had the nerve to get out there and try to do.

The problem with a purpose is that it will continue to nag at you until you listen. It's a little like a voice in your mind, or you could say that it's like the angel and devil on your shoulder.

You want to go for it, and it's something you would love to achieve, but a little voice keeps saying in one ear that it's just too hard, there's too much work to do, you'll never get there. However, there is another voice in the other ear that is whispering a little quieter, saying "what if?" "What if you do it, what if you achieve it?"

Battling the angel and devil is something you need to attempt if you want to be successful. It's not going to be easy, that's for sure. The reason is that that pesky devil is quite loud sometimes and he knocks the angel's volume down with his aggression. The good news is that you can turn his volume down to mute and increase the angel's voice instead. You simply need to pay attention to the inner voice that is telling you to go for it, that perhaps change is what you need.

We can only advise you up to a point. That is what is so difficult about finding your purpose and going for it. Every single person on this planet will have a different purpose or at least a different version of it. Some people might want to change the world, go into activism and work on climate change, whilst others might have more modest views, and perhaps want to try and travel and see the world. Both are equally as valid and equally as worthwhile because they're yours and yours alone.

The first step is acknowledging what your purpose is and understanding how to go about trying to fulfil it.

The next couple of chapters are going to be full of positive pep-talking and advice. We've held your hand so far, and now we just need to solidify the will to make a change. The journey you need to go on is personal, so we can't tell you what to do in terms of specifics; it's too far-ranging and who knows what your journey is about. How to overcome problems and to keep going however are what I have given you advice about constantly. Listening to that advice will see you go far.

Assessing Your Journey

It's very easy to get lost and lose your way on any type of journey, metaphorical or otherwise. One wrong turn and you could end up ambling all over the place, not really sure where you're going. For that reason, it's a good idea to check in and assess your journey occasionally.

Call it a review, a check-in, an assessment, whatever name you want to put on it, but reviewing where you are and how you're doing is a good idea.

As we just mentioned, it's very easy to go off course occasionally and you might not have the first clue that you've done it. Whilst there should always be room for flexibility and spontaneity, as we talked about earlier, sometimes you don't know that you've veered away from where you need to be until you sit down and actually have a long, hard think.

So, how should you do this assessment?

You don't need a pen and paper and you don't need a clipboard, you just need to be able to think honestly and openly with yourself. Perhaps sit down one evening with a glass of wine and have a good, hard think.

Do you feel like your journey is going as you thought it would? Do you feel like you're making progress? Are you feeling empowered and confident, or do you feel something else entirely?

The reason for this assessment is because the way you plan something initially isn't always the way it needs to be. You've never travelled this road before, so how can you be expected to get it right the first time? And, the only way you can identify these mistakes is by sitting down and being honest with yourself about how things really are.

There are more ways to achieve something than you know. The way you have identified might have looked great on paper, and it might have seemed okay to you at the start, but when you look back on a few months, you might understand that you're just not feeling it anymore. Perhaps it's draining your energy; maybe you've tried to take on a little too much.

By sitting down and being honest with yourself about your journey to date, you can make changes and therefore feel better about things.

Ask yourself these questions:

- How do I feel about my journey?
- Is it fulfilling me?
- Do I have time to enjoy my social life and simply just 'be', or am I always trying to work towards something?
- Do I feel healthy and happy?
- Do I think this could be done in a different way?
- Do I still want this purpose to be fulfilled or am I starting to think that maybe I jumped too soon?

If you feel like you've made a mistake, if you feel like things aren't going as well as you'd hoped, or if you've changed your mind completely, all of this is fine. What isn't fine is not being honest with yourself and continuing on with something which isn't giving you the outcome or feels you wanted it to give you.

However, the chances are that when you sit down and look back over your journey so far, you'll feel a sense of achievement and accomplishment. This can turn out to be a motivator because it kickstarts a sense of pride that you should have had from the start. Much of the time, you only realise how far you've come and what you've achieved when you sit down and think about it. By that point, you'll be motivated to continue onwards because you'll want the feeling to increase.

When you're on the way to something, it can also be very easy to try and rush your way through it, but this type of journey is something that is going to take time. You can't think about your purpose and then click your fingers, boom! It's yours! It doesn't work like that, and the reason is that the struggle is part of the journey.

You have to feel difficulties and problems in order to realise how much you want something. If life was easy, we would never appreciate anything, and we'd take the whole thing for granted. How can you be proud of yourself or happy about what you've achieved if you don't have to work for it a little?

By overcoming issues, you can create a sense of resilience and strength which will stand you in good stead in all areas of your life.

How often should you do these reviews? Not too often, but don't leave them too late either. It really depends on how long it's going to take you to achieve what you want or reach your potential. If your journey is a long one, you should probably do a review maybe once a year. If your journey is a short once, check-in every few months and see how you're going. This will keep you firmly on track.

What if You Change Your Mind?

Ah, the million-dollar question!

What if you change your mind halfway through your journey and realise that your purpose isn't as important to you as you thought it was?

In essence, that's fine as long as the reason for changing your mind is a good one.

Ask yourself why you've changed your mind. What part of it do you no longer want? Why do you feel that way? It's easy to change your mind because things have got a little difficult, and if that's the case you need to simply change your approach. If you still believe in the overall purpose and if you still really want the end result to come your way, you need to keep going. However, if you really don't feel the same way about the whole journey anymore, if halfway through it's simply not for you anymore, that's fine.

Sometimes life throws events our way, which creates a totally different mindset for us from that point onwards.

For instance, the death of a close family member can be enough to change the way you think and your outlook on life completely. If this is the case, you need to perhaps hit the pause button for a while and see how you feel a few months down the line. As we've mentioned a few times, road bumps come and go and if you're experiencing something like this, you may wish you'd continued with your journey a few months or a year or so in the future.

However, if you've thought about things clearly if you're really assessed your thoughts and your mind, and you know for sure that this simply isn't what you want any more, it's perfectly okay to admit that to yourself. That doesn't mean your journey so far was in vain because you're sure to have learnt something from it. Perhaps it made you a bit more confident, more resilient, or perhaps it simply taught you what you really do and don't want in life.

Every single event in life is designed to teach you something's e it big or small. In this case, you've learnt something pretty big, and now it's time to go back to the drawing board and think about what you really want. This isn't a failing, it's a pitstop along the way, something to learn from.

What Does Your Final Destination Look or Feel Like?

You might be wondering how you're supposed to know when you've reached your final destination. After all, a purpose might not have a material or a solid point of reference. It might be a sense of feeling or a realisation. In that case, you need to know what your purpose is going to be to you once you've achieved it.

Is it a sense of calm? Is it a realisation of something? Is it having learnt something? Or, it is the achievement of an aim? Perhaps it means you've lost the weight you wanted to lose and now you have a healthy BMI. Perhaps it's that you've travelled the world and you feel more enlightened as a result.

Whilst you're making your way through your journey, ask yourself what you think your purpose is going to feel like once you've achieved it. However, it's important that your journey is part of your life's story and that means you need to embrace every single part of it and not treat it as a race or something to tick off a list. If you're trying to do this, it's not your purpose you're finding, it's an achievement of something else.

You can't always identify how something is going to look or feel once it's done because you've never been there, but you can have an idea of what you think it's going to feel like. Have that in your mind and when you start to feel that way, really feel it, then you should question whether you've managed to obtain your purpose or not.

Most people who actually work towards their purpose in life report feeling calm, happy, fulfilled and as though they've actually achieved something major in their life. However, perhaps you'll feel something completely different. Remember, we're all unique.

Some people feel a sense of disappointment when they reach their purpose and aim because they thought it would be a huge fireworks and bunting moment. It's unlikely to be that way and having unrealistic expectations about how something is going to feel once you've achieved it is something you need to manage. It's unlikely that anyone else is going to celebrate with you because this is a personal journey for you and it may not have a solid material ending that can be seen by other people. Some purposes can have that; however, most don't.

Remember, once you finally reach your purpose, when you realise it and feel it, don't expect congratulations and celebrations from others, simply celebrate for yourself, within yourself and know that you've achieved something amazing for yourself.

That's far better than fireworks and bunting anyway!

Can You Have More Than One Purpose?

Sure you can. There are no rules to this purpose business!

It's important to clarify that a purpose isn't a life's calling, or at least it doesn't have to be. So that means you can easily have more than one purpose and that's completely fine. However, you should work on one at a time to avoid confusing yourself and becoming overwhelmed.

If you try and do too much, one purpose is just going to bleed into the other, and you won't notice or feel the achievement once you've got there. It's far better to focus on one thing at a time and then work through another once that is done. This gives you a far greater chance of success too.

Where to Find Help And Support

Everyone needs help sometimes, so if you feel like you need a little assistance or simply someone to talk to, be sure to reach out and find it.

Maybe you're feeling a little low, a little tired, maybe you're struggling with an idea, or you simply want to reach out and have a chat with someone. That's fine and it's part and parcel of being human!

If you're trying to reach something which is quite a niche, why not try and find a mentor to help you. This is someone who is experienced in the same area that you're trying to work towards, someone who has prior experience and knowledge and who can give you advice on the road you're travelling.

You might not immediately know who to ask but think carefully and try to identify someone who you admire, someone who is skilled and who can give you words of wisdom. When you've found this person, pick their brains when you need help and bounce ideas off them when you're not sure of something.

A mentor can be a huge motivator and someone you can lean upon during times of trouble. Of course, this means explaining to them what you want and what you're trying to achieve and they can tell you whether they're in the best place personally to be a mentor to you. Don't take it personally if they say no, perhaps they're busy and in that case, there will always be someone else you can ask.

Of course, friends and family, in general, are always going to be there for you regardless. These people are going to lift you up when you're down, give you a push when you're struggling and make your life that little bit brighter. So, don't hide your journey from them, try and explain what you're trying to do to a friend or family member who you know will understand.

However, don't expect everyone to agree with you either. It doesn't matter if someone criticises what you're trying to achieve, it's not their journey, it's yours. It can be hard when this happens because you want everyone to be as excited about things as you are, but if you are greeted with confusion, derision, or questions, just don't take it personally. In that case, you simply know that a person isn't the one you can lean on during rough times, and you just find someone else.

Hard, but that's human being sometimes.

Points to Take From This Chapter

In this chapter, we've focused on life during and after your purpose has been realised. It's hard to actually know when you've got there sometimes because not all purposes have a solid ending point that you can instantly recognise. That means you need to be mindful of how you're feeling and whether you feel you've achieved all you can or not.

It's also important to realise that you can change your mind and that it's totally fine if you do. However, you have to be sure of your motivation and know that you're changing your mind because you really want to and not because things have got a little tough.

The main points to take from this chapter are:

- Assessing your journey as you go through it is a good idea, but this doesn't mean you need to sit down and review things every week! A quick check-in with yourself occasionally will give you the answers you need on whether your journey is going how you would like it to or not
- It's possible to completely change your mind on your journey, and if you really do want to change your mind and change course, that's a personal decision that only

you can make. However, be sure that you're not changing your mind simply because things have got a little difficult
- Knowing what your purpose feels like once it's fulfilled can be difficult, but you will usually feel more uplifted and positive when you get there. Don't expect a party; however, this is a personal realisation and not one which everyone may want to celebrate
- It's possible to have more than one purpose in your life, but you should work on one at a time to avoid overwhelming yourself
- Help and support are out there if you want it, but not everyone may share your views. Remember that you don't need validation from anyone else but yourself
- A mentor is a great idea if you're working towards something which is quite a niche. In that case, seek out someone who is experienced and skilled in the area that you're trying to work towards.

Chapter 7:
Will Your Purpose Fulfil You Completely?

We're almost at the end of our book now and by this point, you should be feeling quite uplifted and ready to literally change your life.

Fulfilling your purpose will bring you a huge sense of confidence and happiness in your life and will allow you to enter into the power of who you're supposed to be. However that all hinges on you choosing the right purpose in the first place!

Your purpose may not fulfil you completely, because as we mentioned in our last chapter, it could be that you have more than one purpose. A purpose in the conditions of this book also doesn't add up to a life's calling, because not everyone has one of those.

Some people feel a sense of what they want to achieve from a very young age. For instance, someone may feel that they want to work within the church or another religious place of worship because that is their calling that brings them joy and fulfilment. Another person may feel that they want to go into nursing because they are intrinsically pulled towards helping others and taking away suffering.

You may not feel that way about anything and that doesn't mean there is anything wrong with you at all. In reality, very few people feel a pull or a calling to anything, and if you do feel that, you could argue that you're quite lucky. For most people, it's a case of working towards a purpose, rather than a calling. That means knowing what you want and being willing to head off on a journey to try and get it.

This chapter is going to wrap up the main points of a purpose, so you're not left with any unrealistic expectations about the journey you're going to embark upon. From there, our final chapter will summarise the main ways you can ensure your motivation remains on point. Some of those points might have been covered before, but consider it a reference chapter, a section that you can refer to quickly whenever you're feeling like your will is wobbling a little and you're not sure whether to carry on or not.

What if Your Purpose is Never Fulfilled?

We don't want to bring the doom and gloom here, but we have to answer the question. What if your purpose is never actually fulfilled? What if it has no endpoint and it's a story, a journey that goes on?

In that case, the journey is your purpose, your journey is the entire point, and what you learn and experience throughout it is what you're supposed to learn.

It's vital that you enjoy every step of your journey towards whatever you're trying to reach. Sometimes we're so focused on the end result that we don't take the time to see what is around us. A good way you can learn to appreciate every step of the way is through a technique called mindfulness.

Mindfulness is about living in the present moment and being aware of everything that is going on around you, without allowing your mind to jump back to the past or leap into the future.

Far too often we spend time lamenting the things we did in the past, perhaps living in regret and wishing we could change things. The problem is, you cannot go back in time and change anything; all you can do is make peace with the past and vow not to allow the future to follow suit if what you're looking back on is negative.

Similarly, if you're looking back on something positive, you can enjoy the memory for sure, but you shouldn't try and emulate a moment. It has passed, nothing can replace it and nothing can give you the same type of emotion. Instead, focus on creating new memories and new experiences. That is what your journey is going to give you.

We often think too far ahead too. You might be confused as to how you're supposed to stop yourself from thinking about the future when this very book is about finding your purpose and working towards it throughout your life, planning out your journey and your life's story. In truth, it's very hard not to try and imagine your future on a constant basis, but you need to remember that the moment you're in right now is all you have.

Whilst you're planning for the future, you're working hard, and you're determined to make it work, there are no guarantees in life. You might work hard for something and find that it's going to take you a little longer to get there because you've hit a major road bump along the way. In the meantime, you're not enjoying the moment and you're therefore effectively going to end up living in regret.

We all want to live in the moment, but actually managing it is hard. In terms of your purpose journey, you have to enjoy every day and live in the moment because your purpose may take a long time to fulfil, or it may be that your entire journey is your purpose. In that case, you need to be in it, in order to really feel it.

Mindfulness meditation is a great technique to help you find your focus and awareness in the here and now and to avoid those living in the past moments or jumping into the future. If you hear the word 'meditation' and panic, wait a second. This isn't the same type of meditation that you might be used to, although it does require you to be focused and aware.

Many people worry about trying meditation because it can be hard to master at first. You need to be very in the moment and able to switch off the noise in your head, which is very hard the first few times you try it. However, mindfulness meditation is a little different because not all of the meditation exercises that fall into this category require you to lay down and focus on a specific visualisation. It can be done whilst you're walking around.

Mindfulness increases the more you do it, so give this exercise a try:

- Walk to work instead of driving or catching public transport one time and dedicate a little time to mindfulness
- Head off on the most scenic route you can find and for the first few minutes, focus on your breath, to calm you down. Make sure you put your phone away and put it onto silent to stop it dragging your attention towards it
- Notice your chest rising and falling with each inhalation and exhalation
- When you're calm, simply look around you and pay attention to the scene you're in
- Notice every single sense and what kick them into action; notice the wind in the trees and how it sounds, notice the temperature and how it makes you feel, notice the scent in the air
- Anything which stands out, focus on it. This could be a dog running in the park, a bird tweeting in a tree, someone jogging, it can be anything, but the idea is you're focused on the smaller details
- Don't just see things, but make sure that you're really seeing them; notice the colours, the size, the shape, the sounds, everything about whatever you're seeing. Really appreciate the details.
- Stay in this state and notice as much as you can until you reach your destination

The more you do this, the easier you will find it to zone in on the here and now and shut out all the noise about the tasks you need to complete on your to-do list and the stuff you wish you hadn't done yesterday but somehow did.

Mindfulness is a very useful tool in general and in terms of increasing your emotional intelligence, it's a real deal-breaker. Of course, we're talking about how to change your life's story and go on a journey that leads you towards your purpose. Mindfulness can help you with this because it will train your mind to stay in the here and now and stop you jumping backwards or forwards. That will allow you to enjoy the journey and you'll be able to learn so much more from it as a result.

Why Having a Purpose is Important in The First Place

Let's rewind for a second here. Why exactly is it important to have a purpose in life? Why not just rumble through life and see how things go? Why not just go with the flow and see what happens next?
Because if you don't try anything, nothing will happen. Doors don't just magically open for you; opportunities don't magically fall into your lap. You have to do the groundwork and be willing to accept what comes your way. You might notice an opportunity on the horizon and not realise that you have to do a certain something or show a certain amount of willingness in order for it to move closer to you. By staying still and not doing anything, you miss out completely.

This is what happens when your life doesn't have a specific purpose.

Now, as we've mentioned several times throughout this book, your purpose can be anything you want it to be. It doesn't have to be Earth-shattering, it doesn't have to be something which is going to change the planet, it doesn't have to be anything which is going to make a difference to another person if you don't it to - it has to be personal to you.

Your purpose is what makes your life worth it; it's what gives it meaning. Sure, your family and your friends are huge in that regard too, but you cannot live your life entirely through other people. Your purpose gives you something that pushes you through the hard times in life, something which makes you smile, something to give you determination and something which helps you to feel like your entire life actually means something that you're capable of more than you realise.

Far too many people bumble from day to day and don't try anything. They simply believe that 'what will be, will be'. Now, sure, some things are destined, and whether you believe in fate or not, certain things are going to come your way occasionally. They might be negative, they might be totally positive, but the positive events will be far less prevalent if you don't get up and do something.

It's also easy to identify a purpose but then not do anything about it. That is what this entire book is about - finding a way for you to make headway on reaching your life's purpose and your aims that you want to achieve. You can say "I want ..." but how are you going to get there? What are you going to do to bring that closer to you?

We all have a certain sense of entitlement and some more than others. The thing is, you're not entitled to achieve your aims in life just because you want them. You have to do something to make them a reality. Simply showing up doesn't mean anything is going to come your way; you need to put forth the effort and make things happen.

By following the advice in this book, you'll be far more able to tick those boxes and make opportunities come your way. You'll create chances, and as long as you choose the right ones, you'll find that your purpose moves closer to you as you take more steps towards it.

If you don't have a purpose, does that mean your life is wasted? Of course not! But, it does mean that it will have less meaning.

When you have a purpose in life, you have something to aim towards and something to focus on. It pushes you through and helps you to achieve your potential and become happier and more fulfilled. However, the journey towards that purpose is just as important as the realisation. The things you learn along the way help to shape who you are and what you stand for. By being more mindful of the journey you're on, by doing your best to stay in the here and now with mindfulness techniques, you'll find it far easier to stay on track.

Helping Others Along The Way is Important Too

A final point, before we get onto our final chapter on how to keep yourself going when things get tough, is that if you can help others along the way, that's something you should most definitely do.

When you do good deeds, you feel good about yourself, but if you believe in karma, they come back to you too.

Whatever your purpose is, never trample over someone else to get it. That invalidates everything positive about your journey and your overall focus. It means that you're not being true and you're pushing someone else in front of the bus in order to reach where you want to go. That isn't going to make you feel good about yourself and you'll find fewer people are keen to help you as a result.

However, if you do what you can to help others along the way, you'll develop a greater sense of confidence, happiness, and you're doing good deeds, which is never a bad thing.

Of course, this doesn't mean you have to dedicate yourself to changing the lives of others on a daily basis; it can simply be the odd good deed here and there. Perhaps you can volunteer at a charity that is linked with the purpose you're working towards. This will give you experience in that niche or field and give you more experience and knowledge, whilst allowing you to give something back. The people you meet along the way are also invaluable.

Never underestimate how much power the people you meet whilst on your journey may hold over your final destination and the quality of your overall journey.

One day, you might need to ask someone for advice and when you think back on who to ask, someone you met at a charity gig, or at a benefit rally could be just the person to hold the answers to your query. Treat everyone you encounter throughout your journey as someone who has a huge amount of value - because, they do. Every single person on this planet is valuable, but in terms of your journey, you might need to call upon them in the future.

That doesn't mean you should see everyone as potentially valuable to your cause, but it does help to remember that the people you meet on the way up, might very well be the people who can help you on the way back down.

It's a life lesson that everyone stands to learn, but if you're working towards something, even more so.

You can use this tactic as a rather selfish motivation technique too. You might think that using something for your own gains isn't the best reason, but in this situation, it's win-win all around, so there's no harm! By doing small deeds for others when you're struggling with motivation or confidence, you'll find that you automatically receive a small boost of your own.

You see, when you do something for another person, even if you just help an old person over the road, or you help a struggling mum pack her bags at the supermarket when her toddler is screaming and her other child is running all over the place, you'll feel a sense of having done well. The other person gets a little help; you get the feels.

There's no downside. When you feel this way, you're automatically more likely to get on and do something positive, and in this case, you could use it to continue working towards your journey and realising your purpose. It's a great way to get out of confidence slump and it will make you feel wonderful about yourself too.

Points to Take From This Chapter

This chapter has rounded up the discussion we've had so far about purpose, journeys and your life story. In our next chapter, we're going to give you a quick recap on how to keep going when things are tough, as we mentioned, a quick reference guide, if you will.

However, this chapter has been equally as valuable because it has taught you a few mindset approaches which you need to have in order to remember why you're on this road to progress in the first place.

The main points to take from this chapter are:

- It's important to have a purpose in life because otherwise you might info yourself simply stumbling aimlessly and never feeling fulfilled
- Opportunities and chances don't simply fall into your lap, you need to do some groundwork and make things happen, whilst having the good judgement to understand which opportunities to take and which to allow to pass for the time being

- Feeling fulfilled may not be a trumpet blowing moment, but it will be a sense of happiness and contentment
- Living in the moment is important and this is something which mindfulness meditation can help you with
- Mindfulness meditation isn't the same as the regular type of meditation you might be used to and as a result, many people find it easier to grasp
- You can use mindfulness anywhere and it simply allows you to become more appreciative of the here and now and helps you to live in the moment
- Helping other people along the way will allow you to feel more confident and will give you a boost of motivation.

Bonus Chapter:
Motivation Summary 101

We've taught you everything we can about changing your life's direction, finding your purpose and making headway towards it, but this chapter is going to give you motivation when you need it the most.

Throughout your journey, your story, or whatever you feel more confident calling it, you'll have problems with motivation occasionally. This is something we've explored in detail throughout the book. However, when those moments occur, you don't have the time or patience to read back through the whole book. These are moments of stress, impatience, lack of focus, and they're downright annoying.

With that in mind, this chapter is going to give you the quick recap tips you need to keep you focused and push you back onto the right track. Print out this chapter and keep it somewhere safe, and when you need it, you can quickly pinpoint the motivation technique that calls out to you the most.

Some of the techniques we've already talked about and covered, some are new. Regardless of whether or not these techniques have been covered, this chapter is designed to be a quick read, quick reference guide. Hence why it is called our final bonus chapter.

Remember, changing your current position in life isn't going to be a quick process. You're where you are now and not happy with your position because you've allowed yourself to become stuck. Don't beat yourself up about that now, it happens to countless people the world over. However, what needs to set you apart from those who stay stuck is that you're going to pick yourself, you're going to put a plan in place, and you're going to set off on the journey that takes you where you want to go, rather than leaving you stuck somewhere which isn't fulfilling your or making you feel like you have your whole life ahead of you.

What Does a Lack of Motivation Feel Like?

Before we get into these strategies, how do you know when you're low in motivation? How do you know it's the motivation that's the problem and not something else?

The good news is that when anything else is wrong, e.g. your confidence needs a boost, you're procrastinating, or you're simply tired, working on your motivation can have a knock-on effect on the other areas of your life which might be taking a battering.

When you're low in motivation, you find it hard to concentrate, you can't focus, you'd rather do anything but the thing you're supposed to be doing, and you're just tired, lacking in energy and feeling a little on the resultant to do anything side of things.

You might also not know how to start something, or maybe feel like you're not good enough to do it and that you're better off not doing it because you'll fail.

You see, motivation and confidence are very closely linked, and when one falls, the other tends to be affected too. Energy levels can also drastically affect your motivation.

For that reason, make sure you look after yourself and listen to your body. If you're feeling low in confidence, ask yourself why. Is it because you feel you're not good enough? If that's the case, challenge that thought and ask why that's the case. Even the most famous achievers in the world have gone through periods of time when they felt that very same way, but it's about picking yourself up, dusting yourself down and believing you can do it, even if there doesn't seem to be much proof to work alongside that thought.

A lack of motivation will basically feel like you're swimming in mud. You're stuck. You're overwhelmed. You're stressed. You just don't know which way to turn and that as a result leads you towards procrastination. We don't have to talk about how damaging that can be, we've already covered it!

By understanding what a lack of motivation feels like, you can diagnose yourself with that very problem and then do something about it. The good news is that there are many ways you can boost your motivation quite naturally, and that's what we're going to talk about in our next section.

10 Ways to Keep Your Purpose Journey on Track

This is the section you need to print out and keep! This section is going to talk about ten very tried and tested ways to keep your purpose on track via constant motivation. Again, some of these we've already covered but for completeness' sake and to give you a cut and out and keep section to refer to when you need it, let's go over them again and throw in some new endeavours to keep your brain sharp.

It could be that not every one of these suggestions works for you. Everyone is different, so you might need to try them all and then decide which you're going to keep using and which you're going to just decide aren't for you. Either way is fine, as long as by the end you have a go-to set of tricks you can use to overcome motivation problems.

The tricks we're going to talk about are:

1. Take a break when you need one
2. Focus on your health and wellbeing
3. Remain positive at all times
4. Break your task down into smaller milestones
5. Set small goals which are measurable
6. Remind yourself of your purpose
7. Visualise the end goal
8. Find a mentor or a role model
9. Try delayed gratification
10. Try time challenging yourself

Let's explore each one in turn and explain a little more.

Take a Break When You Need One

No matter how much you might want to believe it, you are not superhuman! From time to time, you might need a break from focusing on your journey and your purpose, and you might simply want to just chill out and enjoy 'being in the moment'. If that's the case and if you really feel a little exhausted from focusing for so long, give yourself the break you need.

This is part and parcel of self-care, but it's equally as important for motivation. When you return back to your journey and your purpose, which you must ensure you do, you'll notice that you're more focused and more energised to continue.

However, you have to be careful that your break doesn't turn into an extended one which goes on for months or even years. You need to set yourself an end time to allow yourself to get back on track.

How can you tell if you need a break? Your mind and body will be screaming at you. Your motivation will be on the floor and you'll just feel very tired. Listen to your body and listen to how you feel. If the idea of having a break simply won't go away, perhaps that's because it's something you need to work towards and then go back to focusing as before.

During your break, make sure that you do things you enjoy and things which make you smile. If you try and focus on working hard on something else, you'll find that you're not energising yourself at all and you're simply tiring yourself out even more. Relax, rest, and then get back to it.

Focus on Your Health And Wellbeing

A good way to get your motivation back on track is to have a quick look at your health and wellbeing. Are you nourishing your body and mind with the foods and drinks it needs, are you giving yourself enough downtime to relax? Do you exercise regularly? How much sleep are you getting? Are you drinking enough water?

It might sound crazy, but a glass of water and a quick break for five minutes can often be enough to energise the mind and if that works when you're at work, how about for your purpose?

Focus on a healthy, varied diet, make sure you're getting plenty of vitamins and minerals and that you're getting at least 7-8 hours of sleep every night. If sleep is a major issue for you, which for many people it is, make that a priority to look at why. Are you too wired before you go to bed because you've been using social media, watching action films or listening to heavy music? Focus on relaxation instead! Try a hot bath, a milky drink, and avoid eating a heavy meal for around 4 to 5 hours before you sleep.

You should also check your sleeping environment to make sure it's comfortable and not too hot, not too cold, etc. The smallest of details can affect how well you sleep or otherwise, but you should never underestimate the power that sleep can have on your motivation levels.

When you're well-rested and full of energy, you're far more likely to be able to hit the motivation button and keep going then you simply want to sit down for a rest. However, when you're tired and sluggish, giving up is a far more attractive and much easier option.

Remain Positive at All Times

Do you remember a few chapters ago we talked about how to reframe your negative thought into positive ones? That's something we need to revisit here in terms of how that can impact on your motivation levels.

When you have a positive mindset, you have an almost natural 'can do' attitude and that can push you on to keep going when you might be feeling like you'd rather not. You're more likely to see the advantages in not giving up in this case. However, if you have a negative attitude, you'll simply think 'what's the point?' In that case, you'll give up and kick yourself for it later on.

Reframing is a great way to boost that new positive mindset and keep it going, the more you reframe your negative thoughts and turn them into positives one instead, the more your mind will learn to see positives before negatives. As we mentioned earlier, the human brain's default setting is negative before positive, so you need to do some brain rewiring work to change that around.

To recap, when you have a negative thought, acknowledge it and then come up with a positive alternative. Repeat it and use visualisation to picture the positive image rather than the negative one. The more

you repeat it, the more your mind will learn to recognise it.
That's reframing in a nutshell, but the power of a positive attitude should never be underestimated and this is certainly something you can use to overcome motivation dips at any point, with anything.

Break Your Task Down Into Smaller Milestones

Again, this is one we've touched upon, but it's an ideal go-to for when your motivation is low. It's hard to get started with any task, and equally as hard to keep going, when the task is so big that you don't seem to be making much recordable headway. If you can't see progress, you're going to be discouraged from the ongoing effort.

However, when you break a task down into smaller milestones and you have something small to work towards, you're more able to keep going because you can see where you're going and what you're doing.

So, take a large task or a large chunk of your journey and work out where you can separate it into milestones. When you achieve one, celebrate it, and then get started on the next one. However, don't become complacent and think that because you've made a little progress you can afford to simply give up and stop. You can't. If you want to complete the task and move forward towards your journey's end and your purpose fulfilment, you have to keep going, whether fast or slow.

Set Small Goals Which Are Measurable

This particular strategy is slightly different from the milestone one we just talked about. It could be that what you're trying to achieve isn't one set, large task. It might be that you simply want to keep making progress in general. In that case, you need to set yourself SMART goals.

This means your goals are:

S - Specific
M - Measurable
A - Attainable
R - Relevant
T - Timely

Basically, SMART goals mean setting aims that are clearly specified without confusion. That they're able to be measured for progress, they're realistic and attainable, and that they're relevant to what you're trying to achieve. This means that whatever goal you set is actually going to help you move towards the bigger picture and what you're trying to achieve in the long-term. The final part means that you have a set timescale in which you're going to achieve the goal.

How you measure a goal completely depends upon the goal itself and what it is. Some goals are easier to measure than others, but SMART goals tend to be small and short in terms of their timescales.

By doing this, you're able to see progress, and you'll feel like you're getting somewhere. This in itself is very motivating, so if you're finding that you're stuck trying to swim through mud, change your approach and set a SMART goal. Once you've achieved that one, set another, and before you know it, you'll be ticking off goals left, right, and centre!

Remind Yourself of Your Purpose

It's very easy to lose sight of what you're trying to achieve from time to time, especially when life gets in the way. In this case, you need to regularly find yourself of your purpose and do it in a way that is visual, so you're more pushed to continue on with it.

How about a mood board? This means collecting images of what you're trying to work towards and arranging them almost in a scrapbook style. This is something you can look at and add to whenever something comes to mind. Then, when your motivation is struggling a little, you can spend some time with your mood board and feel inspiration strikes once more.

If that isn't working for you, how about a mantra. This could be a statement of intent that you repeat over and over whenever you feel your will and your motivation wavering. For instance, if you've decided that you want to become a teacher, but it means retraining and going to university, you're probably going to question your decision and have a few wobbles occasionally. This is because the size of the purpose you're working towards is very large, but it certainly doesn't mean it's unattainable.

Your mantra, in this case, could be "I am driven to teach, I will reach my aim". This is motivating and it reminds you of what you're trying to do.

A mantra can be anything and as with the positive affirmations we talked about earlier, it simply needs to be something you believe in and something you can connect with on a deep level. You need to then repeat the mantra over and over in order to solidify your belief. Whenever you feel yourself struggling with motivation, close your eyes and say it aloud. If you aren't in a space in which to do this, you can say it quietly in your mind but the act of actually verbalising the words does make a stronger connection with your inner will and motivation, so that is the best way forward if you can.

Visualise The End Goal

We talked a huge amount earlier on about visualisation, but you should never underestimate the power of this strategy. We did cover this in a huge amount of detail earlier on, so we will simply summarise here and give you a quick reference guide, if you need something to remind you of how to use visualisation if your motivation is wavering.

The reason this strategy is so useful in these types of situations is because it reminds you of what something might feel like when you have achieved it.

When you use visualisation, you first need to set the scene and that means spending a little time really meditating on the thing you're trying to achieve. Sit somewhere quiet and make sure you're not going to be disturbed. Make sure you're not going to be disturbed and first turn attention to your breath. When you're ready, try and picture the thing you're trying to achieve at the point when you've actually got there, you're right at the summit.

Imagine what it feels like, tastes like and looks like. The more detail you can add, the stronger your visualisation exercise will be. You need to spend time doing this quite a lot at the start, but then you can simply call upon the image whenever you feel your motivation starting to waver.

Try and remember how it felt, and that positive feeling, that sense of accomplishment will be enough to motivate you towards notably continuing on, but also potentially increasing your will to achieve it too.

Find a Mentor or a Role Model

Having someone you can talk to when your motivation might be low, or someone you can chat with when you're not sure about something is a vital part of keeping yourself moving towards your final aims and fulfilling your purpose.

Not everyone will be able to use this strategy because not every type of purpose requires the use of a mentor, however, a role model doesn't necessarily have to be connected with the thing you're working towards; it can be someone who you like to spend time with because they have an infectious personality, someone who is always positive and upbeat. Spending time with a person like this will rub off on you and help you to feel more upbeat and positive too.

A mental is ideal for people who have a purpose within a specific niche. For example, we talked a short while ago about someone who might want to retrain as a teacher. In that case, a mentor such as a university lecturer, an experienced teacher you know well, or someone who has been down a similar path as you and who has also changed career direction, could be a great source of motivation and advice.

Identifying this type of person shouldn't be difficult for you, and depending upon the route you're going down, you simply need to find someone, ask them if they'd mind being your sounding board and then be sure not to bother them too much! Remember, your mentor isn't someone who make decisions for you, it's someone who you ask for advice when you're not sure of something; use that opportunity wisely, but don't overdo it.

Try Delayed Gratification

You've probably tried delayed gratification in the past for something or another, most people have. Whilst the jury is out on whether it is the most effective way to get something done, it certainly works for many people and in that case, it's worth trying if you're finding your motivation going south.

Delayed gratification is a great way to avoid procrastination. So, if you're struggling to get going and you keep putting something off, promise yourself a reward, but don't give it to yourself until you've fulfilled the thing you need to do.

For example, let's use the training to be a teacher example once more. In this case, you will be doing university work and it might be difficult for you to get back into education after a break. This could mean that essays and other written work are a difficult side of the game for you. In that case, you might want to put off writing an essay because you're struggling to focus or you're not sure how to tackle it.

Rather than not doing it and therefore jeopardising your university grade, which has serious implications for your new future career, promise yourself a reward when it is finished. Of course, the size of the reward needs to be proportionate to the task you need to complete. Don't promise yourself a two-week-long Caribbean cruise just to finish an essay! However, you could promise yourself and your partner or friend a meal out that evening, or that weekend.

By promising yourself something which you want and something you're going to look forward to and enjoy, you're pushing yourself to want to do it. The more you focus on the thing you're going to reward yourself with; you're stronger your desire to finish it.

However, do not give in and allow yourself to have the reward if you don't complete the task. The rules of delayed gratification have to be followed in order to make it an effective motivation booster.

Try Time Challenging Yourself

Our final option is time challenging. This is actually a time management technique that is very useful when you're starting to procrastinate with something. In this case, you would look at the task you need to do or the thing you need to complete in order to move forward on your journey towards your purpose, and then you would identify a specific amount of time in which you're going to complete it.

The thing to be mindful of here is being realistic. Make sure that you choose a timescale that is doable otherwise you're simply setting yourself up for failure. Using the essay example from our last point - if the essay is going to really take four hours, tell yourself that you're going to complete it in three hours and fifty minutes, and then work flat out to do it. When you achieve it, reward yourself.

This method is effective because it taps into your competitive side, and everyone has one of those! You want to win, you don't want to let yourself down by not reaching your time aim, and that is going to push you forward to complete whatever it is that is causing you the procrastination or lack of motivation issue.

Anyone who wants to make progress in their lives, anyone who wants to work towards their aims, change their story, make progress with their journey and fulfil their purpose, and have to learn how to motivate themselves when they're struggling to find it. These ten methods will certainly do that for you, so print this page out and use it as a reference when you might be starting to feel sluggish, slow, and in danger of procrastinating.

Made a Mistake? Try This

Everyone makes mistakes. Nobody is perfect, and as we mentioned before, what is perfectionism anyway?

However, when you realise that you've made a mistake, perhaps you've taken a wrong turn or made a bad decision, you have to acknowledge it quickly and learn from it.

If you feel like you might have taken a wrong turn, sit down and analyse it. Don't beat yourself up and don't blame yourself. Remember, this is a journey, and no journey is perfect. Part of the charm is to get lost occasionally, but it all hinges on finding yourself again.

Avoid blame games and negativity as these are not going to help you. Instead, see every situation such as this as a learning curve. What made you move toward that mistaker misjudgement? How can you recognise it in the future, so you don't do the same thing again?

What can you learn? That is the main thing you need to ask yourself.

Rather than sitting down and berating yourself, telling yourself how terrible you are and wondering how you could have been so careless, tell yourself that mistakes are for learning from and that everyone has to make errors in order to do better next time.

Blame will not help, education will.

Points to Take From This Chapter

This chapter is designed to be something you can print out and use if you feel like your motivation is starting to waver. A few of the strategies have been talked about before, a few are new, but they're all important enough to recap at this point.

You will not achieve what you want in life, and you will not realise your purpose unless you keep motivation on your side. The problem is that motivation doesn't always want to play the same game as you! In that case, a few ways to force it towards your side is vital. The ten strategies we've mentioned are therefore key things to try.

The main points to take from this chapter are:

- Motivation ebbs and flows naturally, but you can force it to play your game by learning strategies to boost it whenever needed
- Procrastination is dangerous, but you can avoid it by understanding this point and learning how to motivate yourself whenever you're struggling
- A lack of motivation often feels like swimming through mud, and it can be hard to shake if you're not sure how to do it
- It's normal to make mistakes occasionally, and you shouldn't beat yourself up about these
- Find a learning opportunity in every error you make.

Conclusion

And there we have it!

We're now at the end of our book and by this point, you should be feeling brimming with ideas and hope that you can finally turn your life around and shake off the comfort zone.

It's very easy to get stuck in life and it's far easier to stay where you are than it is to make changes. The problem is, if you don't wake up and smell the coffee, so to speak, you're going to find yourself several years down the line looking back on things and wondering whether you should have done it all differently. Regret is not something that is pleasant to live with.

A purpose isn't a life's calling, that's something we've mentioned a few times. A purpose can ebb and change, you might have more than one purpose, but it's basically a reason for doing something, a desire to achieve something and do better. A purpose is never a negative thing, it's always a positive thing to work towards, something to motivate you on towards bigger and better things in your life.

However, you need to be sure that the purpose you identify is actually yours and it's not that you've chosen someone else's idea. This is a common route, usually when someone is struggling with feeling stuck in their life but they're not sure which way to go. By choosing any old purpose, they feel like they're making headway, but it's always going to come back and bite them; you can't walk someone else's path or go on someone else's journey, you can only live your own story and your own life.

A little careful thinking is required before you embark on any changes. Think carefully about what you want and be sure to really know how it's going to affect and benefit you in the future.

Once you know what you want, it's time to start planning your journey to get there. This is part of your purpose, so never simply rush it and try and get there as fast as possible. The things you learn and encounter throughout your journey will help you learn and will also effectively change you too. You'll become more confident, more focused, more intent on what you want. It isn't possible to go through a journey like this and not be changed by it in some way. Don't worry, these will all be positive changes!

We should address at this point that makes changes is always scary. If you're feeling nervous or apprehensive, don't worry it's all perfectly normal. Fear is the reason why we stay in our comfort zones because we know what's going to happen there; we know how things are going to affect us and how we're going to feel. We stay there because it is literally as comfortable as it sounds.

The thing is, comfort isn't fulfilling, it isn't going to teach you anything, and it's not going to stretch you and show you what you're truly capable of. It's only going to show you what you're missing.

You're also going to worry that you've made the wrong choice, you're going to question yourself, and you're going to make mistakes. Again, all of this is totally normal and not something which should cause you to seriously question your actions. However, if you really do feel like you've chosen the wrong purpose or the wrong journey, that's something which you need to question carefully. Mistakes are sent our way in order to educate us and allow us to learn. See every problem that comes your way as an opportunity in this way and you'll never fall short.

All that's left to say now is good luck.

We hope that the contents of this book have proven useful and that you're feeling motivated by our words. The single biggest message to take from this book is that you do not have to live a life that is unfulfilling for a second longer. There are other options, but you do need to be brave enough to take the first step towards realising them.

Every single person on this planet has more potential within them than they know, you included. By making a point of actually thinking about what you want and going for it, you're building your own confidence and allowing yourself a far better chance at a life which gives you a sense of accomplishment.

Do not allow yourself to live with regrets, do not sit there thinking "what if" for a second longer. Life is to be lived, but it's not going to fall in your lap either. The effort will be worth it, no matter how long your journey lasts for. Also, you should remember to enjoy every single part of your journey too and not simply rush to the final element that is supposed to signal your purpose being fulfilled.

There are countless lessons to be learnt, there are many skills you need to unearth, there are several people you need to meet along the way, and there are more opportunities out there than you can even comprehend right now.

Give yourself a push, follow our advice, motivate yourself and just go for it. It will be the single best decision you ever make in your life, but not allow yourself to give up before you're through. Keep going, even if you need to take a break.

What's more important to you - living in your comfort zone and being safe, or getting out there and living your life, finding out what is really possible and what rewards might be available to you?

You know the answer already, don't you?

A Short message from the Author:

Hey, are you enjoying the book? I'd love to hear your thoughts!

Many readers do not know how hard reviews are to come by, and how much they help an author. Reviews alone are what typically makes my book stand out in the crowd, persuades another person to choose this book.

I would be incredibly grateful if you could take just 60 seconds is all it takes to write a brief review - even if it's just a few sentences – on whatever bookstore or marketplace you purchased this book from!

Thank you for taking the time to share your thoughts!

More from Jean-Claude Leveque

-Conquer your Emotions
-Conquer your Concentration
-Conquer your Motivation
-F*ck Anxiety
-F*ck Panic Attacks

www.ingramcontent.com/pod-product-compliance
Lightning Source LLC
Chambersburg PA
CBHW031118080526
44587CB00011B/1029